Collins **wild guide**

Butterflies & Moths

John Still

HarperCollinsPublishers Ltd.
77-85 Fulham Palace Road
London
W6 8JB

The Collins website address is: www.collins.co.uk

Collins is a registered trademark of HarperCollinsPublishers Ltd.

First published in 1996

10 09 08 07 06 05

10 9 8 7 6 5 4 3 2 1

A catalogue record for this book is available from the British Library.

ISBN 0-00-719151-0

Edited and designed by D&N Publishing
Colour reproduction by Colourscan, Singapore
Printed and bound by Printing Express Ltd, Hong Kong

WHY BUTTERFLIES AND MOTHS?

Just what is it about butterflies and moths that makes them so popular? They have had more books written about them than any other member of the animal kingdom, except birds. Gardening, photography and wildlife magazines all regularly produce illustrated features on how to attract, photograph or study these insects. They are regular guests on television wildlife programmes, sometimes even having a whole programme to themselves. There are even butterfly 'centres' (enclosed gardens for mainly tropical butterflies and moths) and 'farms' (places for breeding and studying butterflies) around the world – almost every country now has at least one of these.

So what exactly is it that they have that other animals do not? Well, clearly they are beautiful. Many butterflies have bright and colourful patterns, making them extremely attractive. Moths, of course, are thought of as terribly dull, poor things, but are they really? Take a look at the Elephant Hawkmoth (p.181) and you will see that it is more colourful than many butterflies. You have to remember that most moths rest during the day, and need the sort of colours, greys and browns, that will help them hide, but that does not make them any less beautiful if you look at them carefully.

Butterflies and moths are also small and accessible, which means that they are easy to watch or study. Keeping caterpillars in captivity, for instance, takes up very little space, and this makes them an ideal subject for schools to study.

Finally, they come in many shapes, sizes and colours. Each kind, or species, looks different as an adult, but they also have different eggs, caterpillars, chrysalids and cocoons. They each go through different stages at different times of the year, each feeding on different kinds of plants. All this variety means that they do not have to compete with one another for the same foods, and it is this, more than anything else that has made butterflies and moths, together with most other insects, one of the more successful forms of life on this planet.

WHAT ARE BUTTERFLIES AND MOTHS?

In the eighteenth century a Swedish naturalist called Carl Linné thought up a way of dividing the world's animals in to **groups**, such as mammals, reptiles, insects and others. Each one of these groups he then divided further, so that insects, for example, were separated into dragonflies, flies, beetles, bees, and others. These groupings were divided again into **families**, such as Swallowtail butterflies, and from there into individual **species** (types). This system of latin names, now used by all naturalists, is called **classification**. There are around 20,000 species of butterflies in the world, and about 150,000 species of moths, and together they make up the second largest group of insects (the largest group is beetles).

Like most other insects, butterflies and moths have six legs, two eyes, a pair of **antennae** (feelers) and a body divided into three parts: head, **thorax** (chest) and **abdomen** (stomach). What makes them different from other insects is that they have four wings covered with tiny scales, each one a single colour, and it is these scales, arranged in rows like tiles on a roof, that give their wings such amazing patterns.

So what makes a butterfly different from a moth? The easiest answer to this question is ... nothing! The division between them has no real scientific value, and in some countries they are all called butterflies, but this is not going to help you, so... There are several general rules to work out the differences, all of them having exceptions. Usually, butterflies fly during the day, have clubbed antennae and fold their wings vertically over their backs, while moths have straight or feathery antennae, fly at night and keep their wings flat. The trouble is that while no butterfly has feathery antennae, some moths have clubbed antennae, and quite a few moths fly during the day. Also, some moths do fold their wings over their backs, just as some butterflies keep theirs flat.

Butterflies and moths all have four stages to their **life cycle – egg, caterpillar, pupa** (also known as chrysalis) and **adult** – and the transformation that takes place within the pupa is called **metamorphosis** (complete change). Some other insects, such as grasshoppers, have only three stages – egg, nymph and adult – where the nymph looks like a miniature adult without wings and the chrysalis stage is missed out altogether; this is known as **incomplete metamorphosis**. Each species of butterfly or moth takes a different length of time to go through the life cycle. For example, a species living in the far north of Europe, where summers are very short, may take two years to develop, while a species living around the Mediterranean coast may complete the cycle two or three times in a year, each new generation being known as a **brood**.

In Europe, most butterflies and moths have to **hibernate** (sleep) through the winter, but they do not all do this at the same stage in the life cycle. The Small Tortoiseshell, for example, hibernates as an adult, but the Common Blue does so as a caterpillar. In really hot summers, particularly around the Mediterranean, some species may become temporarily dormant until the weather cools a little. When they do this, it is called **aestivating**.

Butterflies and moths have many enemies, and so different species have evolved different ways to avoid being breakfast or lunch for a passing bird or other predatory animal. The commonest way is **camouflage**, blending into a background of leaves or bark. Moths are particularly good at this. Some species, such as Burnet moths, are poisonous, and they are brightly coloured as a warning that they do not taste very good. Caterpillars may have hairs or spines, to make it difficult for most birds to eat them. Some caterpillars live together in communal tents, spinning large silk webs over several leaves, coming out only to feed or to make the 'tent' bigger. A few caterpillars, such as those of Blues and Hairstreaks, are protected by ants in exchange for a sweet and sticky liquid they are able to produce on which the ants feed. These are just a few examples that help to show the endless variety of which these insects are capable. Reading this book should help you to find a lot more.

HOW TO USE THIS BOOK

There are more than 500 butterfly species in Europe, and several thousand moth species, which makes it a little difficult to decide which species to include in a book of this size. This book, however, like the others in this series, is mainly for beginners and is designed to be easy to use, so only the commonest butterflies and moths that are resident in Europe have been chosen. By leaving out the less common species (even if they are more attractive) and those that **migrate** (travel from other countries or continents), it is hoped that you will be able to more easily identify those that you find.

At the top of each page is a small silhouette which represents the general shape and colour of the family to which the species on that page belongs. These are as follows:

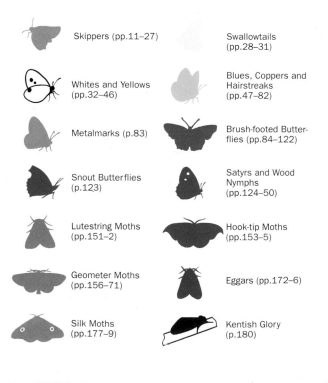

Skippers (pp.11–27)

Swallowtails (pp.28–31)

Whites and Yellows (pp.32–46)

Blues, Coppers and Hairstreaks (pp.47–82)

Metalmarks (p.83)

Brush-footed Butterflies (pp.84–122)

Snout Butterflies (p.123)

Satyrs and Wood Nymphs (pp.124–50)

Lutestring Moths (pp.151–2)

Hook-tip Moths (pp.153–5)

Geometer Moths (pp.156–71)

Eggars (pp.172–6)

Silk Moths (pp.177–9)

Kentish Glory (p.180)

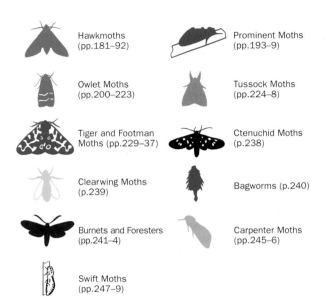

Hawkmoths (pp.181–92)

Prominent Moths (pp.193–9)

Owlet Moths (pp.200–223)

Tussock Moths (pp.224–8)

Tiger and Footman Moths (pp.229–37)

Ctenuchid Moths (p.238)

Clearwing Moths (p.239)

Bagworms (p.240)

Burnets and Foresters (pp.241–4)

Carpenter Moths (pp.245–6)

Swift Moths (pp.247–9)

The symbol of the sun or moon indicates whether the insect flies by day or night, or, in some cases, both.

The **photograph** on each page shows the butterfly or moth as you are most likely to see it. For example, Grayling butterflies almost always sit with their wings shut, so this is what the photograph shows. If the female is very different from the male, or identification is helped by looking at the underside (the view of a butterfly with its wings closed), the **illustration** will show this. The illustrations mainly show both upperside and underside (undersides are marked ▲). If the sexes are very similar, then the caterpillar is shown.

Not all butterflies and moths are easy to identify. This book deals only with **type species** (the normal insect), but there can also be **subspecies** (other races). For example, the Swallowtail butterfly has a British subspecies with much darker markings than the European type species. Although space does not allow for illustrations of any subspecies, if there are any then some mention is made, where possible, in the text. To confuse things further, there can also be **seasonal variation**, where the summer brood of a species such as the Map butterfly looks quite different from the brood that hatches in spring.

The main text will tell you in which part, or parts, of Europe the butterfly or moth can be found, and in what sort of **habitat** (type of countryside) it is most likely to be seen. It will also describe the caterpillar, if it is not illustrated, mention if there is more than one brood each year, and include any other information that may be useful or interesting. Above the main text, at the top of each page, the **family** to which each species belongs is given.

The **ID Fact File** gives the following information at a glance:

Wingspan: is the measurement from wing tip to wing tip with the wings out flat.

Description: contains a brief summary of the colours and patterns of the species, mentioning any special features that may make identification easier.

Hibernating Stage: tells you at which point of the life cycle the species sleeps through the winter. How long it sleeps for cannot be given, because that depends on weather conditions; a cold autumn will cause an insect to go into hibernation early, while a warm spring will cause it to wake up earlier.

Flight Period: shows when the adult insect may be seen flying and does not include hibernating periods.

Caterpillar Food Plants: are the sorts of plants the caterpillars may be found feeding on, but you will probably have to look very carefully. A quick look at this section will show you how fussy butterflies can be compared to many moths.

Lookalikes: where included, refer to any other species in the book that may look similar to the one you are examining.

Finally, there is the **time bar**, a quick month-by-month guide to when you can expect to find the adult insects. Unlike the Flight Period section in the ID Fact File, this includes the winter months that any species may be hibernating through. All you have to do now is go out and start looking for your first butterflies and moths.

FINDING BUTTERFLIES AND MOTHS

The most obvious place to start looking for butterflies is in your own garden, or, if you do not have one, your local park. You will soon find that butterflies are attracted to certain types of flowers, where the nectar on which they feed is easily available. Flowers such as roses and dahlias are quite useless to them.

You will not find many different species, because only a few have adjusted to the change from countryside to towns and cities. Most of the smaller butterflies, like many of the blues and skippers for example, live in small colonies and never fly very far from the area in which they were born. Other butterflies, such as the Painted Lady, fly long distances, never staying in the same place for very long, and these are the ones you are most likely to find first.

Moths will be a little more difficult, because they will be hiding away during the day. The best places to look for them are on tree trunks and sheltered fences, but at night they are often attracted to lights, so try looking around street lamps and doorways that have been lighted during the night, as the moths may be resting nearby.

Finding moths at night can sometimes be easier if you have the right flowers to attract them into your garden. *Buddleia*, for instance, is as attractive to moths as it is to butterflies. Another way to see them is to shine a torch or other bright light on to a white sheet and see if any are attracted to the light.

Keeping adult butterflies or moths in captivity can be tricky because they need plenty of space to fly about in, and butterflies will need sunshine to keep them warm. Caterpillars, on the other hand, are very little trouble. A simple jam jar will be enough to keep one or two in, as long as you can change their food every day. Never stand it in sunlight, though, or you will kill your caterpillars!

Once you have learnt to recognise the butterflies and moths in your neighbourhood, then you are ready to try further afield.

HABITATS AND CONSERVATION

Moths are fairly easy-to-please insects; because most of them fly at night, they do not need the sun to create the right conditions for them, and their caterpillars can often eat a wide variety of different plants, which means that they usually do not need any particularly special habitats. Butterflies, though, are specialists. Some like the cool shade and dappled sunlight of woodlands, others prefer the wide open spaces of grasslands and heathlands. All butterflies are limited by the plants eaten by their caterpillars, which sometimes makes them **locally common** (common only in suitable areas). The Scarce Copper (p.72), for example, eats dock, which is a common plant, but prefers damp situations near streams, so it is only found where the plant and the habitat are combined. Therefore, to find new butterfly species you will have to visit different habitats.

When naturalists first started to study butterflies and moths, they did so by collecting them. This involved killing the insects and spreading their wings out on special boards until the bodies had dried. The specimens could then be stored in glass-covered drawers and preserved for years. The Natural History Museum in London has many hundreds of thousands of specimens stored in this way, some of them now very old.

Specimens are still collected today by some people, and single examples of rare species can sometimes change hands for quite a lot of money. However, more people are becoming aware of our disappearing wildlife and the need for conservation, and so they are slowly turning to photography, which can often be a more challenging and rewarding, though sometimes frustrating, way of collecting.

Like most wildlife, butterflies and moths now need all the help they can get if they are to survive. Encouraging them into your garden, by growing the right food plants for them, is a simple but effective way of doing this. There are, for example, six butterfly species in Europe that feed on stinging nettle, as well as a number of moths, so just growing this in a sheltered, sunny place may help to bring you a garden full of butterflies next summer.

J	F	M	A	M	J
J	A	S	O	N	D

Mallow Skipper
Carcharodus alceae

ID FACT FILE

WINGSPAN:
2.3–3 cm

DESCRIPTION:
Marbled brown ground colour. Forewings have 3 small whitish bands forming a rough broken triangle. Underside much paler. Hindwing edge clearly scalloped. Sexes alike

HIBERNATING STAGE:
Caterpillar

FLIGHT PERIOD:
Spring to late summer

CATERPILLAR FOOD PLANTS:
Mallow (*Malva*) and related plants

LOOKALIKES:
Dingy Skipper (p.15)

A butterfly of warm, dry, flowery hillsides, and fairly common in central and S Europe. There are usually two, sometimes three, broods in a year in warmer areas, and the adult may be seen on the wing almost continuously through the summer. In colder regions (higher up in the mountains) there will be only one brood, flying around June. Caterpillars feed mainly at night and pupate in leaf-litter.

caterpillar

HESPERIIDAE (SKIPPERS)

J	F	M	A	M	J
J	A	S	O	N	D

Tufted Marbled Skipper

Carcharodus flocciferus

ID FACT FILE

WINGSPAN:
2.5–3 cm

DESCRIPTION:
Marbled brown
ground colour
marked with
whitish spots.
Underside much
paler with notice-
able tuft of dark
hair under the
forewing. Hind-
wing edge slight-
ly scalloped.
Sexes alike

**HIBERNATING
STAGE:**
Caterpillar

FLIGHT PERIOD:
Summer

**CATERPILLAR FOOD
PLANTS:**
Horehound
(*Marrubium*) and
woundworts
(*Stachys*)

LOOKALIKES:
Marbled Skipper
(p.13)

This butterfly is common in central and S
Europe, where it can be found in dry, flowery
grassland and other rough open areas, mainly
in the hills and mountain districts up to 2000 m.
It is much less common in the lowlands. The
caterpillar lives in a shelter made by drawing
a leaf or two together, as do most Skipper
caterpillars, and probably feeds at night; but
little is known of this species otherwise.

J	F	M	A	M	J
J	A	S	O	N	D

Marbled Skipper
Carcharodus lavatherae

ID FACT FILE

WINGSPAN:
2.5–3.2 cm

DESCRIPTION:
Marbled brown to
olive-brown
ground colour
marked with
white spots and
streaks. Easily
recognised by a
row of arrow-
shaped white
spots along the
edge of the hind-
wings. Underside
very pale.
Hindwing edge
scalloped. Sexes
alike

**HIBERNATING
STAGE:**
Caterpillar

FLIGHT PERIOD:
Early summer

**CATERPILLAR FOOD
PLANTS:**
Woundworts
(*Stachys*)

LOOKALIKES:
Tufted Marbled
Skipper (p.12)

Although widespread through central and
S Europe, this butterfly is very local; it is
usually found on the dry, flowery grasslands
of limestone hills, up to around 1500 m. There
is usually only one brood each year, very rarely
two, and the caterpillar lives in the usual
shelter of a leaf or two, moving down to the
ground to pupate in the leaf-litter in late
spring.

HESPERIIDAE (SKIPPERS)

J	F	M	A	M	J
J	A	S	O	N	D

Chequered Skipper
Carterocephalus palaemon

ID FACT FILE

WINGSPAN:
2.2–2.8 cm

DESCRIPTION:
Dark brown
marked with dark
orange-yellow
spots. Underside
much paler, with
spots picked out
in light brown.
Sexes alike

**HIBERNATING
STAGE:**
Caterpillar

FLIGHT PERIOD:
Late spring to
early summer

**CATERPILLAR FOOD
PLANTS:**
Grasses, particu-
larly brome
(*Bromus*)

A widespread but local butterfly, found mainly
in open woodland and nearby meadows in
NE and central Europe. It is now extinct in
England, but is still to be found in a small area
of Scotland. The caterpillar lives in a tube
made from a single blade of grass and, when
fully grown, hibernates in the same kind of
shelter, pupating in the spring, in a cocoon
amongst grasses.

caterpillar

J	F	M	A	M	J
J	A	S	O	N	D

Dingy Skipper
Erynnis tages

ID FACT FILE

WINGSPAN:
2.3–2.6 cm

DESCRIPTION:
Dark grey-brown with darker brown spots forming 2 rough bands across the forewings; small white dots in a neat row along the edge of each wing. Underside pale plain fawn with only white dots for markings. Sexes alike, but female slightly paler

HIBERNATING STAGE:
Caterpillar

FLIGHT PERIOD:
Late spring to early summer

CATERPILLAR FOOD PLANTS:
Bird's-foot-trefoil (*Lotus*) and related plants

LOOKALIKES:
Mallow Skipper (p.11)

This moth-like butterfly is common throughout most of Europe with the exception of the far north. It prefers sunny banks and hillsides, up to around 2000 m, that have an abundant supply of flowers. At rest the adult will fold its wings in typical moth fashion, close around the body. The caterpillar always remains within a shelter made by drawing several leaves together, and makes a cocoon when pupating in the spring.

caterpillar

HESPERIIDAE (SKIPPERS)

J	F	M	A	M	J
J	A	S	O	N	D

Silver-spotted Skipper
Hesperia comma

ID FACT FILE

WINGSPAN:
2.5–3 cm

DESCRIPTION:
Orange-brown
framed by dark
brown borders;
pale spots just
visible, more so
on the female.
Male easily
recognised by
black sex-brand
on forewing. In
both sexes,
underside pale
olive-brown with
silvery white
spots

**HIBERNATING
STAGE:**
Egg

FLIGHT PERIOD:
Summer

**CATERPILLAR FOOD
PLANTS:**
Grasses, but par-
ticularly sheep's-
fescue (*Festuca*)

LOOKALIKES:
Large Skipper
(p.18)

This butterfly, though widespread throughout
most of Europe, is confined to areas with chalky
soils, where it prefers grassy meadows and
hillsides up to around 2500 m, usually in areas
where the grass has been grazed. The olive-
green caterpillar has a large black head and feeds
mainly at night, spending the day within the
shelter of a rolled grass blade. It makes a coarse
cocoon at ground level in which to pupate.

left male
right female

HESPERIIDAE (SKIPPERS)

Large Chequered Skipper
Heteropterus morpheus

J	F	M	A	M	J
J	A	S	O	N	D

ID FACT FILE

WINGSPAN:
3–3.5 cm

DESCRIPTION:
Dark brown with small orange-yellow spots near leading edge of forewings. Underside forewings similar, but hindwings have black-ringed white spots on yellow. Female recognised by broad fringe along wing edges

HIBERNATING STAGE:
Caterpillar

FLIGHT PERIOD:
Summer

CATERPILLAR FOOD PLANTS:
Various grasses

This butterfly is quite unmistakable, looking like no other species in Europe; and though it is not rare, it is not especially common. It is found mainly across central Europe, but in France only in the north and west. There is a preference for open woodland, but it can also be seen in both dry and damp grassy meadows, mainly in the lowlands. The caterpillar is greyish-white, with black and white stripes and a brown head.

left male
right female

HESPERIIDAE (SKIPPERS)

| J | F | M | A | M | J |
| J | A | S | O | N | D |

Large Skipper
Ochlodes venatus

ID FACT FILE

WINGSPAN:
2.5–3.2 cm

DESCRIPTION:
Uppersides very similar to Silver-spotted Skipper, but female spotting much darker. Undersides also similar but lacking the silvery spots

HIBERNATING STAGE:
Caterpillar

FLIGHT PERIOD:
Summer

CATERPILLAR FOOD PLANTS:
Various grasses

LOOKALIKES:
Silver-spotted Skipper (p.16)

This butterfly is common throughout most of Europe, but is absent from the northern parts of the continent, including Scotland. It is usually found on grassy hillsides, and also around forest edges and roadsides, up to about 2000 m. The green caterpillar is striped with darker green down the back; it is yellow at the sides and has a large dark brown head. It pupates within a cocoon amongst grass blades. Up to three broods in the south.

male

female

HESPERIIDAE (SKIPPERS)

J	F	M	A	M	J
J	A	S	O	N	D

Large Grizzled Skipper
Pyrgus alveus

ID FACT FILE

WINGSPAN:
2.5–3 cm

DESCRIPTION:
Dark grey-brown with white spots on forewings. Underside of forewings similar, but hindwings pale greenish-brown with large white spots. Female similar but larger

HIBERNATING STAGE:
Caterpillar. Egg in Scandinavia

FLIGHT PERIOD:
Late spring to summer

CATERPILLAR FOOD PLANTS:
Cinquefoils (*Potentilla*), bramble (*Rubus*), and related plants

LOOKALIKES:
Olive Skipper (p.23)

This is very much a mountain butterfly, and is absent from the lowland countries, the British Isles and N Scandinavia. It is commonly found in flowery meadows, rarely below 1000 m or above 2000 m. The green caterpillar has a dark, almost black, head, and feeds mainly at night. Pupation takes place in a flimsy cocoon at ground level amongst leaf-litter. In Scandinavia, hibernation has been found to take place in the egg stage.

male

HESPERIIDAE (SKIPPERS)

Oberthur's Grizzled Skipper

Pyrgus amoricanus

ID FACT FILE

WINGSPAN:
2–2.5 cm

DESCRIPTION:
Dark grey-brown with slightly paler spots on hind-wings and white spots on forewings. Undersides olive-brown with white spots. Sexes alike

HIBERNATING STAGE:
Caterpillar

FLIGHT PERIOD:
Summer in the north, late spring and late summer in the south

CATERPILLAR FOOD PLANTS:
Cinquefoils (*Potentilla*) and wild strawberry (*Fragaria*)

This butterfly is common right across central and S Europe, but absent from the north, including the British Isles. It prefers dry flowery open spaces such as fields, meadows and embankments in lowland areas, but can be found up to around 1500 m. There is only one brood in northern parts, but usually two further south. The second generation produces slightly smaller adults. The caterpillar pupates in a rolled up leaf.

caterpillar

J	F	M	A	M	J
J	A	S	O	N	D

Safflower Skipper
Pyrgus fritillarius

ID FACT FILE

WINGSPAN:
2.7–3.3 cm

DESCRIPTION:
Dark grey-brown
with white spots
on forewings,
darker, less
distinct spots on
hindwings.
Underside similar
but white spots
on forewings
more extensive;
ground colour
on hindwings
olive-brown.
Female similar
but slightly larger

**HIBERNATING
STAGE:**
Caterpillar

FLIGHT PERIOD:
Late spring to
late summer

**CATERPILLAR FOOD
PLANTS:**
Safflower
(*Carthamus*),
mallow (*Malva*),
and cinquefoil
(*Potentilla*)

This is a common, sometimes abundant,
butterfly, found locally throughout most of
central and S Europe. It prefers dry, sunny
and flowery meadows up to around 2000 m.
Interestingly, although there seems to be only
one brood each year, the adults can be seen all
through summer, suggesting that emergence is
staggered. The olive-green caterpillar has a
large dark brown head and draws the food
plant leaves together to form a shelter.

HESPERIIDAE (SKIPPERS)

J	F	M	A	M	J
J	A	S	O	N	D

Grizzled Skipper
Pyrgus malvae

ID FACT FILE

WINGSPAN:
1.8–2.2 cm

DESCRIPTION:
Dark grey-brown
with white spots.
Underside similar
but paler. Sexes
alike

**HIBERNATING
STAGE:**
Pupa

FLIGHT PERIOD:
Spring to
summer

**CATERPILLAR FOOD
PLANTS:**
Wild strawberry
(*Fragaria*),
cinquefoil
(*Potentilla*), and
related plants

LOOKALIKES:
Red-underwing
Skipper (p.24)

This little butterfly is probably the commonest
of the Grizzled Skippers, found everywhere
except Ireland, Scotland and N Scandinavia. It
is a butterfly of grassland and open spaces,
damp or dry, up to 2000 m, wherever there is a
profusion of wild flowers, and can often be seen
sunning itself on a patch of bare earth. There
are two broods each year in warmer areas, only
one in the north and at higher altitudes.

caterpillar

J	F	M	A	M	J
J	A	S	O	N	D

Olive Skipper
Pyrgus serratulae

ID FACT FILE

WINGSPAN:
2.2–2.5 cm

DESCRIPTION:
Very similar to
Large Grizzled
Skipper, the
main differences
being apparent
on the underside
of the hindwings,
where the white
spots are slightly
smaller, and the
ground colour is
browner

**HIBERNATING
STAGE:**
Caterpillar

FLIGHT PERIOD:
Summer

**CATERPILLAR FOOD
PLANTS:**
Cinquefoils
(*Potentilla*), and
lady's-mantle
(*Alchemilla*)

LOOKALIKES:
Large Grizzled
Skipper (p.19)

This butterfly is common throughout central
and S Europe, though absent from Portugal
and W Spain. It is an uplands species, rarely
found below 1000 m, and prefers grassy
meadows with plenty of flowers up to around
2400 m. The green caterpillar has a dark brown
head and lives within the shelter of a rolled-up
leaf, pupating in a cocoon at the base of the
food plant. There is only one brood a year.

male

female

HESPERIIDAE (SKIPPERS)

Red-underwing Skipper
Spialia sertorius

ID FACT FILE

WINGSPAN:
2.2–2.4 cm

DESCRIPTION:
Similar to Grizzled Skipper, but white spots smaller. Easily identified by underside of hindwings, where the ground colour is reddish-brown. Sexes alike

HIBERNATING STAGE:
Caterpillar

FLIGHT PERIOD:
Late spring and late summer

CATERPILLAR FOOD PLANTS:
Bramble (*Rubus*), cinquefoil (*Potentilla*), and related plants

LOOKALIKES:
Grizzled Skipper (p.22)

This is a widespread and fairly common butterfly, found across most of central and S Europe, where it prefers rough, open spaces up to around 2000 m. There are normally two broods each year, and the second generation usually produces slightly smaller adults. Several sub-species have been named. The caterpillar lives in a folded leaf, feeding mainly at night, and when fully grown pupates at ground level amongst leaf-litter.

caterpillar

HESPERIIDAE (SKIPPERS)

Lulworth Skipper
Thymelicus acteon

ID FACT FILE

| J | F | M | A | M | J |
| J | A | S | O | N | D |

WINGSPAN:
2.5–2.8 cm

DESCRIPTION:
Male orange-brown with lighter spots and black sex-brand on forewings; female darker with no sex-brand. Underside plain orange-brown

HIBERNATING STAGE:
Caterpillar

FLIGHT PERIOD:
Late spring to mid-summer

CATERPILLAR FOOD PLANTS:
Grasses, particularly brome (*Bromus*)

This little butterfly is found in small colonies throughout most of central and S Europe, and also in England where it is confined to a few areas in Devon and Dorset. It prefers grassy meadows and hillsides up to around 2000 m, and is easily attracted to flowers. Newly hatched caterpillars go into hibernation straight away, eating no more than their eggshell until the following spring. They pupate when fully grown in a loose cocoon amongst grass.

female

male

HESPERIIDAE (SKIPPERS)

Essex Skipper
Thymelicus lineola

ID FACT FILE

WINGSPAN:
2.2–2.6 cm

DESCRIPTION:
Bright orange-brown finely edged with dark brown. Underside similar but paler; hindwings particularly, have slightly yellowish tinge. Male has black sex-brand on forewings. Female slightly larger

HIBERNATING STAGE:
Egg

FLIGHT PERIOD:
Summer

CATERPILLAR FOOD PLANTS:
Various grasses

LOOKALIKES:
Small Skipper (p.27)

This butterfly is common throughout most of Europe, but is absent from N Scandinavia. In the British Isles it can be seen only in parts of S England. It is normally found in open grassy places, like hillsides and meadows, up to around 2000 m. The caterpillar is green with a darker stripe down its back, and pale yellow stripes along the sides. It lives within a rolled grass blade and feeds mostly at night, pupating in a small cocoon when fully grown.

female

male

HESPERIIDAE (SKIPPERS)

J	F	M	A	M	J
J	A	S	O	N	D

Small Skipper
Thymelicus sylvestris

ID FACT FILE

WINGSPAN:
2.4–2.7 cm

DESCRIPTION:
Almost identical to Essex Skipper. Best identified by examination of the tip of the antennae, which in this species is pale orange-yellow underneath, while that of the Essex Skipper is black

HIBERNATING STAGE:
Caterpillar

FLIGHT PERIOD:
Summer

CATERPILLAR FOOD PLANTS:
Various grasses

LOOKALIKES:
Essex Skipper (p.26)

This is one of the most abundant of the Skippers, found almost everywhere except Ireland, Scotland and Scandinavia. It prefers open grasslands and meadows up to around 2000 m. The eggs are laid in small clusters and, when hatched, the tiny caterpillars immediately make a cocoon in which to overwinter, separating and feeding in the spring, when they are usually most active at night. Pupation takes place in a flimsy cocoon amongst grass blades.

caterpillar

PAPILIONIDAE (SWALLOWTAILS)

J	F	M	A	M	J
J	A	S	O	N	D

Scarce Swallowtail
Iphiclides podalirius

ID FACT FILE

WINGSPAN:
6.4–8 cm

DESCRIPTION:
Creamy white
with black
stripes and long
black tail. Blue
crescents and
red spot on hind-
wings. Underside
similar. Sexes
alike

**HIBERNATING
STAGE:**
Pupa

FLIGHT PERIOD:
Late spring and
mid-summer in
the south, early
summer every-
where else

**CATERPILLAR FOOD
PLANTS:**
Sloe (*Prunus*),
and related
Prunus trees

This is actually a fairly common butterfly
throughout most of central and S Europe. It
is constantly on the move, with no special
territory, but is most often seen in the
lowlands, only rarely flying in areas as high as
around 2000 m. Because of their food plants,
they are often seen flying around orchards.
The colour of the pupa normally matches that
of its background, so that usually it is green in
summer and brown in winter.

caterpillar

Swallowtail
Papilio machaon

ID FACT FILE

WINGSPAN:
6.4–7.6 cm

DESCRIPTION:
Pale yellow with black markings. Blue crescents and a red spot on the hind-wings. Underside similar, slightly paler. Sexes alike

HIBERNATING STAGE:
Pupa

FLIGHT PERIOD:
Mid-spring to mid-summer, depending on locality; 1–3 broods

CATERPILLAR FOOD PLANTS:
Fennel (*Foeniculum*), carrot (*Daucus*), and related plants

This butterfly is common throughout most of Europe except the far north-east of Scandinavia and Finland. In the British Isles it is restricted to the fens of E England. Everywhere else it prefers flowery meadows up to around 2000 m, but it keeps on the move, never staying in one place. The newly hatched caterpillar is black and white, looking like a bird-dropping, and changes colour as it grows. The pupa may be either green or brown.

caterpillar

PAPILIONIDAE (SWALLOWTAILS)

J	F	M	A	M	J
J	A	S	O	N	D

Apollo
Parnassius apollo

ID FACT FILE

WINGSPAN:
7–8.4 cm

DESCRIPTION:
White and shiny, slightly transparent at the edges, with large black spots on the forewings and 2 large red spots on the hindwings. Underside similar with red patch near body. Sexes alike

HIBERNATING STAGE:
Caterpillar

FLIGHT PERIOD:
Mid-summer

CATERPILLAR FOOD PLANTS:
Stonecrop (*Sedum*)

This is a mountain butterfly, found throughout Europe on all the main mountain ranges up to around 2000 m. It prefers flowery meadows and mountain pastures, and Scandinavia is the only region where it is seen in the lowlands. It is very variable with many named subspecies. The caterpillar will feed only when the sun is shining enough to warm the air, and when fully grown it pupates on the ground in a loose cocoon.

caterpillar

PAPILIONIDAE (SWALLOWTAILS)

Southern Festoon
Zerynthia polyxena

ID FACT FILE

WINGSPAN:
4.6–5.2 cm

DESCRIPTION:
Pale yellow marked with black and red, strong zig-zag pattern at the edges. Underside similar, but hindwings mostly white rather than yellow

HIBERNATING STAGE:
Pupa

FLIGHT PERIOD:
Mid-spring

CATERPILLAR FOOD PLANTS:
Birthwort (*Aristolochia*)

This rather local butterfly is found only in SE Europe, where it prefers meadows and other rough, open places up to around 1000 m. The caterpillar is usually pale pinkish-brown with rows of red warts that have short black hairs at the tips. It is poisonous (tastes nasty), and these colours help to advertise this. The straw-coloured pupa is attached to the food plant and held upright by a thread of silk fastened to the head.

caterpillar

PIERIDAE (WHITES AND YELLOWS)

J	F	M	A	M	J
J	A	S	O	N	D

Orange Tip
Anthocharis cardamines

ID FACT FILE

WINGSPAN:
3.8–4.8cm

DESCRIPTION:
White with black
tips to the
forewings, male
with large orange
patch. Underside
mottled with
black and yellow

**HIBERNATING
STAGE:**
Pupa

FLIGHT PERIOD:
Mid- to late
spring

**CATERPILLAR FOOD
PLANTS:**
Lady's smock
(*Cardamine*),
hedge mustard
(*Sisymbrium*),
and related
plants

This butterfly is common throughout Europe
except S Spain and the far north. It prefers
open woodland, flowery meadows and sometimes gardens, up to 2000 m. The green caterpillar has a white line along each side
and is darker underneath. It feeds on the
flowers and seed-pods of its food plants, and
is also cannibalistic, eating any other eggs and
caterpillars it finds on the same plant. The pupa
is very slender and looks a little like a seed-pod.

male

female

PIERIDAE (WHITES AND YELLOWS)

J	F	M	A	M	J
J	A	S	O	N	D

Black-veined White
Aporia crategi

ID FACT FILE

WINGSPAN:
5.6–6.8 cm

DESCRIPTION:
White, some-
times becoming
slightly transpar-
ent with age;
veins and edges
picked out in
black. Underside
similar. Female
slightly brown

**HIBERNATING
STAGE:**
Caterpillar

FLIGHT PERIOD:
Late spring to
early summer

**CATERPILLAR FOOD
PLANTS:**
Hawthorn
(*Crataegus*), sloe
(*Prunus*), and
related plants

This butterfly is found throughout most of
Europe except N Scandinavia and the British
Isles (where it became extinct in the early
20th century). It is a migratory butterfly and is
always on the move, never staying in one place
for long, and although it is attracted to flowers
it also drinks water from wet ground. The
caterpillars live together in a silk tent until
after hibernation and sometimes become a
pest in orchards.

caterpillar

PIERIDAE (WHITES AND YELLOWS)

Berger's Clouded Yellow
Colias australis

ID FACT FILE

Wingspan:
4.2–5.4 cm

Description:
Very similar to
Pale Clouded
Yellow, but
colours generally
brighter with less
black. Only the
caterpillars are
very different

**Hibernating
stage:**
Caterpillar

Flight period:
Late spring and
late summer,
sometimes early
autumn in the
south

**Caterpillar food
plants:**
Horseshoe vetch
(*Hippocrepis*)
and crown vetch
(*Coronilla*)

Lookalikes:
Pale Clouded
Yellow (p.36)

A fairly common butterfly throughout central
and S Europe, sometimes migrating northwards
as far as S England. It prefers dry, flowery open
grasslands up to around 2000 m. There are
usually two broods each year, but in the south
there may sometimes be a third. The caterpillar
is bluish-green with bright yellow lines down
the back and sides, and rows of black spots. The
green pupa is slightly leaf-like.

male underside

left male
right female

PIERIDAE (WHITES AND YELLOWS)

J	F	M	A	M	J
J	A	S	O	N	D

Clouded Yellow
Colias croceus

ID FACT FILE

WINGSPAN:
4.6–5.4 cm

DESCRIPTION:
Male orange-yellow, edged black, with 1 black spot on each forewing. Female darker (sometimes white) with heavier black markings. Underside yellow

HIBERNATING STAGE:
Caterpillar

FLIGHT PERIOD:
Mid-spring to early autumn; several broods

CATERPILLAR FOOD PLANTS:
Lucerne (*Medicago*), and many related plants

A common butterfly across central and S Europe, often migrating northwards in the spring and summer and reaching as far as S Scandinavia as well as S England. It prefers heaths and other open, flowery grasslands, up to around 2200 m, and is a very fast flier. The caterpillar is green with a yellow line along each side, marked at intervals with a little red streak. The pupa is green and leaf-like.

left male
right female

PIERIDAE (WHITES AND YELLOWS)

J	F	M	A	M	J
J	A	S	O	N	D

Pale Clouded Yellow
Colias hyale

ID FACT FILE

WINGSPAN:
4.2–5 cm

DESCRIPTION:
Male pale yellow, female white, both with black edges and 1 black spot on each forewing, 1 orange spot on each hindwing. Underside yellow

HIBERNATING STAGE:
Caterpillar

FLIGHT PERIOD:
Late spring and late summer

CATERPILLAR FOOD PLANTS:
Lucerne (*Medicago*), and many related plants

LOOKALIKES:
Berger's Clouded Yellow (p.34)

This butterfly is found mainly in central and E Europe, migrating northwards every year to S Scandinavia, sometimes reaching S England. It prefers flowery meadows and fields of clover, generally in the lowlands but up to around 2000 m. The caterpillar is green with a yellow line down each side marked with a series of thin red streaks. There are two broods each year, but although the caterpillar hibernates, it cannot survive the winter in the colder areas of the north.

male underside

left male
right female

PIERIDAE (WHITES AND YELLOWS)

Moorland Clouded Yellow
Colias palaeno

| J | F | M | A | M | J |
| J | A | S | O | N | D |

ID FACT FILE

WINGSPAN:
4.8–5.4 cm

DESCRIPTION:
Male pale yellow, female white, both with broad black edges. Underside yellow (male), or greenish-white (female), greyer near body, with 1 white spot on each hindwing

HIBERNATING STAGE:
Caterpillar

FLIGHT PERIOD:
Early summer

CATERPILLAR FOOD PLANTS:
Bilberry (*Vaccinium*)

This butterfly is found only in central and NE Europe and does not seem to have the migratory urge of other Clouded Yellows. It is one of the commonest species in the north, and prefers peat-bogs and moorland, usually in lowland areas. It has a strong flight, but generally flies only when the sun is strong enough to warm the air. The caterpillar is green with a plain yellow line down each side, and the pupa is green and leaf-like.

male underside

left male
right female

PIERIDAE (WHITES AND YELLOWS)

J	F	M	A	M	J
J	A	S	O	N	D

Dappled White
Euchloe ausonia

ID FACT FILE

WINGSPAN:
3.6–4.8 cm

DESCRIPTION:
White with black tips and a black spot on each forewing. Black and yellow scales on underside make a strong greenish pattern on white. Female darker

HIBERNATING STAGE:
Pupa

FLIGHT PERIOD:
Early summer in the mountains; early and late spring in the lowlands

CATERPILLAR FOOD PLANTS:
Candytuft (*Iberis*) and related plants

This butterfly is found only in S Europe, where it flies in flowery meadows and hillsides up to around 2000 m. There are three main races of this species, two living only in the mountains, and the third, the commonest, living mostly in the lowlands. The caterpillar is green with a white line along the sides, yellowish stripes down the back and tiny black dots all over. The pupa, attached to the food plant, is straw-coloured and looks like an old leaf.

male

female

Cleopatra
Gonepteryx cleopatra

ID FACT FILE

WINGSPAN:
5–6.8 cm

DESCRIPTION:
Similar to
Brimstone but
male has large
bright orange
patch on
forewing; female
has pale orange-
yellow streak on
underside of
forewing

HIBERNATING STAGE:
Adult

FLIGHT PERIOD:
Early to late
spring and early
to late summer

CATERPILLAR FOOD PLANTS:
Buckthorn
(*Rhamnus*)

LOOKALIKES:
Brimstone (p.40)

This butterfly is found only in S Europe,
where it is common and prefers open
woodland, meadows and dry, stony mountain
slopes up to around 2000 m. Its wings have a
leafy shape which provides perfect camouflage
when hibernating in the winter. The caterpillar
is bluish-green with a very pale green line
along the sides, and when not feeding it
usually lies along the middle of a leaf, where it
is well hidden.

male underside

female

J	F	M	A	M	J
J	A	S	O	N	D

Brimstone
Gonepteryx rhamni

ID FACT FILE

WINGSPAN:
5.2–6 cm

DESCRIPTION:
Male bright
yellow, female
greenish-white,
with an orange
spot in the mid-
dle of each wing.
Underside similar
but greener

**HIBERNATING
STAGE:**
Adult

FLIGHT PERIOD:
Early spring to
late summer,
new adults
hatching in early
summer

**CATERPILLAR FOOD
PLANTS:**
Buckthorn
(*Rhamnus*)

LOOKALIKES:
Cleopatra (p.39)

This common butterfly is found throughout
Europe except Scotland and N Scandinavia.
It prefers open woodland and forest edges,
sometimes gardens, up to around 1800 m, but,
like many butterflies in this family, it keeps on
the move, never staying in one place for long.
The caterpillar is green with a pale line along
each side, and lies along the middle of a leaf
when not feeding, which makes it very hard to
find. The pupa is very leaf-like.

female

▲ male underside

PIERIDAE (WHITES AND YELLOWS)

J	F	M	A	M	J
J	A	S	O	N	D

Wood White
Leptidae sinapis

ID FACT FILE

WINGSPAN:
3.8-4.8 cm

DESCRIPTION:
Pure white, male
with black patch
at the tip of the
forewings,
female with pale
grey streaks.
Underside
similar, streaked
with grey

**HIBERNATING
STAGE:**
Pupa

FLIGHT PERIOD:
Mid-spring to late
summer; 1–3
broods, depend-
ing on locality

**CATERPILLAR FOOD
PLANTS:**
Bird's-foot-trefoil
(*Lotus*) and
tuberous pea
(*Lathyrus*)

This little butterfly is found throughout most
of Europe except the far north. In the British
Isles it is found in S England, Wales and
Ireland. It prefers open woodland and forest
edges up to around 2000 m, and has a very
weak, fluttery flight, never flying very far. The
slender caterpillar is green with a bright yellow
line along the sides. When fully grown it leaves
the food plant, usually pupating in a nearby
clump of grass.

female, 1st brood

male, 1st brood

PIERIDAE (WHITES AND YELLOWS)

J	F	M	A	M	J
J	A	S	O	N	D

Large White
Pieris brassicae

ID FACT FILE

WINGSPAN:
5.6–6.6 cm

DESCRIPTION:
White with
forewing tips
black. Female
has 2 black
spots on
forewings. Under-
side similar but
hindwings pale
greyish-green

**HIBERNATING
STAGE:**
Pupa

FLIGHT PERIOD:
Mid-spring to late
summer; 2 or 3
broods

**CATERPILLAR FOOD
PLANTS:**
Nasturtium
(*Tropaeolum*),
cabbage
(*Brassica*), and
related plants

This is probably the most familiar butterfly in
Europe, found everywhere except the far
north, although in summer it migrates even
there. It is found wherever there are flowers
and suitable food plants, which has made it
something of a pest in gardens and agricultural
areas. The caterpillars are green with black
spots and a yellow line along the back and
sides; they live in a group when young and
often wander some distance before pupating.

left male
right female

PIERIDAE (WHITES AND YELLOWS)

| J | F | M | A | M | J |
| J | A | S | O | N | D |

Southern Small White
Pieris mannii

ID FACT FILE

WINGSPAN:
4–4.6 cm

DESCRIPTION:
Very similar to Small White but slightly smaller and with larger black tips to the forewings

HIBERNATING STAGE:
Caterpillar and pupa

FLIGHT PERIOD:
Early spring to early autumn; 3 or 4 broods

CATERPILLAR FOOD PLANTS:
Candytuft (*Iberis*) and related plants

LOOKALIKES:
Small White (p.45)

This butterfly is fairly common in SE Europe, with a few rather local colonies in the southwest. It prefers rough, dry flowery places up to around 1600 m. Adults hatching in summer are usually larger than the spring brood. Unlike other *Pieris*, this is not a migratory species and does not fly very far. The caterpillar is bluish-green with a yellow line along the back and sides and covered with tiny black dots. It can be found at almost any time of the year.

mating pair

left male, 2nd brood
right female, 1st brood

PIERIDAE (WHITES AND YELLOWS)

J	F	M	A	M	J
J	A	S	O	N	D

Green-veined White
Pieris napi

ID FACT FILE

WINGSPAN:
4–5.2 cm

DESCRIPTION:
Very variable.
White with black
tip and 1 black
spot (2 in
female) on each
forewing. Under-
side yellowish
with veins edged
grey. Later
broods larger
and paler

**HIBERNATING
STAGE:**
Pupa

FLIGHT PERIOD:
Early spring to
early autumn;
1–3 broods,
depending on
locality

**CATERPILLAR FOOD
PLANTS:**
Hedge mustard
(*Sisymbrium*) and
many related
plants

This is a common butterfly throughout Europe
and is found almost everywhere, including
gardens, up to around 2500 m. It is always on
the move, never staying in one place for long.
The caterpillar is pale green, covered with
minute black dots, and has a row of yellow
spots along each side. When fully grown it may
wander from the food plant before pupating,
and the colour of the pupa can vary to match
the background.

1st brood male **(left)**
and female **(right)**

J	F	M	A	M	J
J	A	S	O	N	D

Small White
Pieris rapae

ID FACT FILE

WINGSPAN:
4.6–5.4 cm

DESCRIPTION:
White; male has
1 black spot,
female 2, on each
forewing, with
small black tips.
Underside similar
but hindwings
greyish-yellow

**HIBERNATING
STAGE:**
Pupa

FLIGHT PERIOD:
Early spring to
early autumn;
1–4 broods,
depending on
locality

**CATERPILLAR FOOD
PLANTS:**
Nasturtium
(*Tropaeolum*),
cabbage
(*Brassica*), and
related plants

LOOKALIKES:
Southern Small
White (p.43)

This is probably one of the commonest
European butterflies, found almost
everywhere except the far north, to where
it will normally migrate each summer. It can
be seen wherever there are suitable flowers
and food plants, sometimes becoming a pest
in gardens. The caterpillar is green with a pale
yellowish line down the back and a row of
yellow spots along the sides. It may wander
away from the food plant before pupating.

left male
right female

J	F	M	A	M	J
J	A	S	O	N	D

Bath White
Pontia daplidice

ID FACT FILE

WINGSPAN:
4.2–4.8 cm

DESCRIPTION:
White with black markings. Underside similar but hindwings patterned with greyish-green. Female darker

HIBERNATING STAGE:
Pupa, sometimes caterpillar

FLIGHT PERIOD:
Early spring to early autumn; 2–4 broods, depending on locality

CATERPILLAR FOOD PLANTS:
Mignonette (*Reseda*), rock-cress (*Arabis*), and related plants

This butterfly is common in central and S Europe, but migrates northwards every summer, often reaching S Scandinavia, sometimes S England. It prefers flowery meadows, particularly clover fields, and other rough areas, up to 2000 m. The caterpillar is bluish-grey, covered with small black spots, and has yellow lines along the back and sides. The pupa is formed on the food plant and may vary in colour from green to brown.

left male
right female

LYCAENIDAE (BLUES, COPPERS AND HAIRSTREAKS)

J	F	M	A	M	J
J	A	S	O	N	D

Alpine Argus
Albulina orbitulus

ID FACT FILE

WINGSPAN:
2.2–2.7 cm

DESCRIPTION:
Males bright sky
blue with narrow
black margins;
female plain
brown, some-
times blue near
the body. Under-
side greyish with
creamy white
spots. Small
black spot in
centre of
forewings

**HIBERNATING
STAGE:**
Caterpillar

FLIGHT PERIOD:
Summer

**CATERPILLAR FOOD
PLANTS:**
Alpine milk-
vetches
(*Astragalus*)

As the name may suggest, this little butterfly
is very much a mountain species, and is found
only in alpine meadows around the French,
Swiss and Italian Alps, and also in the southern
mountain ranges of Norway and Sweden. It is
rarely seen below 1000 m or above 3000 m.
The plain green caterpillars are very fond of
nibbling the flowers and buds of the food
plant, and this is probably the most obvious
clue to their presence.

caterpillar

male

| J | F | M | A | M | J |
| J | A | S | O | N | D |

Brown Argus
Aricia agestis

ID FACT FILE

WINGSPAN:
2.2–2.7 cm

DESCRIPTION:
Dark brown with
a row of orange
crescents near
the outer edge of
each wing.
Underside pale
greyish-brown.
Orange and white
spots on both
sides; the white
having a black
centre. Sexes
alike

**HIBERNATING
STAGE:**
Caterpillar

FLIGHT PERIOD:
Late spring to
late summer

**CATERPILLAR FOOD
PLANTS:**
Rockrose
(*Helianthemum*),
also crane's-bill
(*Geranium*) and
related plants

LOOKALIKES:
Northern Brown
Argus (p.49)

This is a butterfly of open grassland and
meadows, though rarely above 1000 m. It is
found through most of central and S Europe
except Spain and Portugal; in the British Isles
it is found only in S England, but it is not
especially common. There may be two or three
broods each year, depending on locality. The
caterpillars are tended by ants, and when fully
grown will pupate in spring at the base of the
food plant.

caterpillar

J	F	M	A	M	J
J	A	S	O	N	D

Northern Brown Argus
Aricia artaxerxes

ID FACT FILE

WINGSPAN:
2–2.5 cm

DESCRIPTION:
Very similar to
Brown Argus
except that
orange crescents
on forewings
reduced or miss-
ing. Underside
much paler,
black spots
much smaller.
British sub-
species has
white spot in
centre of each
forewing on
upperside, black
spots mostly
absent from
underside and
ground colour
much darker

**HIBERNATING
STAGE:**
Caterpillar

FLIGHT PERIOD:
Early summer

**CATERPILLAR FOOD
PLANTS:**
Rockrose
(*Helianthemum*),
also stork's bill
(*Erodium*) and
related plants

LOOKALIKES:
Brown Argus
(p.48)

This little butterfly has a rather scattered
distribution, and as a result has produced a
number of different sub-species. It prefers
sheltered grasslands and moorlands up to
around 2200 m, though rarely below 1000 m.
In the British Isles it is found only in N England
and Scotland; in the rest of Europe in isolated
pockets throughout, including Scandinavia. The
caterpillar is similar to the Brown Argus (p.48),
but the lines along the sides are whiter.

male, European race

female, European
race

LYCAENIDAE (BLUES, COPPERS AND HAIRSTREAKS)

J	F	M	A	M	J
J	A	S	O	N	D

Holly Blue
Celastrina argiolus

A common butterfly, found throughout Europe except Scotland and N Scandinavia. It prefers woodland clearings and hedgerows, but is also often seen flying round parks and gardens. There are two broods each year, with adult females showing a marked difference between generations; and second generation adults are strongly attracted to bramble blossoms, otherwise all adults prefer tree-sap and carrion. Caterpillars vary greatly in both colour and pattern.

ID FACT FILE

Wingspan:
2.3–3 cm

Description:
Pale sky-blue, males with thin black edging, females more heavily marked, particularly in second generation. Underside pale blue, almost white, with tiny black spots

Hibernating stage:
Pupa

Flight period:
Late spring and late summer

Caterpillar food plants:
Holly (*Ilex*) in spring, ivy (*Hedera*) in autumn, also a few other shrubs. Usually eats flower buds and berries, sometimes young leaves

first brood male **(left)** and female **(right)**

J	F	M	A	M	J
J	A	S	O	N	D

Small Blue
Cupido minimus

ID FACT FILE

WINGSPAN:
1.8–2.2 cm

DESCRIPTION:
Dark brown,
males with a
little blue colour-
ing near body,
females plain.
Underside very
pale grey-brown
with tiny black
spots

**HIBERNATING
STAGE:**
Caterpillar

FLIGHT PERIOD:
Late spring to
late summer,
depending on
locality and
number of
broods

**CATERPILLAR FOOD
PLANTS:**
Kidney vetch
(*Anthyllis*) and
related plants.
Usually eats
flowers and
seed-pods

Except for S Spain, the Netherlands and parts
of Scandinavia, this little butterfly is found
throughout most of the rest of Europe,
although in the British Isles it lives in small
isolated colonies. It prefers south-facing grassy
banks and slopes up to around 2000 m. There
may be one or two broods each year depending
on the locality and climate. The caterpillars
hibernate in dead flower heads and are
attended by ants. The pupa is usually fixed to
a grass stem.

caterpillar

male

J	F	M	A	M	J
J	A	S	O	N	D

Geranium Argus
Eumedonia eumedon

ID FACT FILE

WINGSPAN:
2.3–3 cm

DESCRIPTION:
Plain dark brown.
Males may have
a suggestion of
blue near the
body, females
sometimes have
faint orange
crescents on
hindwings.
Underside light
brownish-grey
with black spots.
Centre spot on
hindwings
surrounded by
white streak

**HIBERNATING
STAGE:**
Caterpillar

FLIGHT PERIOD:
Summer

**CATERPILLAR FOOD
PLANTS:**
Meadow crane's-
bill (*Geranium*)
and related
plants

This butterfly is fairly common in E Europe,
and while it is absent from Portugal, NW
Europe and the British Isles, it can be found
in a few isolated pockets in Spain, France
and Greece. Although it is possible to see
this butterfly in lowland country, it is really
a hillside and mountain species, preferring
grasslands and other open, sunny places up
to around 2500 m. The caterpillar is tended
by ants.

caterpillar

J	F	M	A	M	J
J	A	S	O	N	D

Short-tailed Blue
Everes argiades

ID FACT FILE

WINGSPAN:
2–2.7 cm

DESCRIPTION:
Male is pale bluish-violet with narrow black edges; female dark brown, often with some blue near body. Second and later broods generally darker. Underside very pale grey-blue, almost white, with tiny black spots. Both sexes have a very small tail

HIBERNATING STAGE:
Caterpillar. Sometimes egg (further north)

FLIGHT PERIOD:
Late spring to late summer

CATERPILLAR FOOD PLANTS:
Medicks (*Medicago*), trefoils (*Lotus*) and related plants. Usually prefers seed-heads

This butterfly is common in central and S Europe, although in Spain it is only found in the north east. In warm summers it will often migrate northwards, sometimes even reaching the British Isles. It prefers damp grasslands and heaths in the lowlands and valleys, rarely above 500 m. There are usually two, sometimes more, broods each year, and the caterpillar is pale green with darker stripes, turning brown during hibernation.

left male
right female

J	F	M	A	M	J
J	A	S	O	N	D

Green-underside Blue
Glaucopsyche alexis

ID FACT FILE

WINGSPAN:
2.3–3.5cm

DESCRIPTION:
Male blue with black edges, female dark brown, usually with a hint of blue close to the body. In both sexes, underside pale grey with single row of large black spots and patch of greenish-blue close to body

HIBERNATING STAGE:
Caterpillar

FLIGHT PERIOD:
Late spring to early summer

CATERPILLAR FOOD PLANTS:
Vetches (*Astragalus*) and related plants

A fairly common butterfly, found throughout most of Europe except the British Isles, Portugal and the far north. Although often seen in lowland areas, it is really a hillside and mountain species, preferring open flowery banks and fields up to around 1300 m. The caterpillar is green with broad yellowish and olive-brown stripes along the back. It is attended by ants, and females actively seek out food plants close to ant nests for egg laying.

mating pair

male

Long-tailed Blue
Lampides boeticus

ID FACT FILE

WINGSPAN:
3–3.5 cm

DESCRIPTION:
Male blue with narrow black edges, female dark brown with blue close to body. In both sexes, underside streaky pattern of pale brown and white, hind-wing having broad white band and 2 small black and blue spots close to the short tail

HIBERNATING STAGE:
Pupa

FLIGHT PERIOD:
Late spring to early autumn

CATERPILLAR FOOD PLANTS:
Many plants from Legume family. Sometimes a pest on peas and other crops

LOOKALIKES:
Lang's Short-tailed Blue (p.68)

This butterfly is common in Africa and much of Asia, so in Europe it lives only in the warmer south, usually migrating northwards each year, although rarely reaching as far as the British Isles. Seldom seen in towns and gardens, this is a butterfly of open, flowery places up to around 2000 m. There are several broods each year, and the caterpillar, which varies in colour from green to pale brown, often lives inside the pods of the food plant.

male underside

female

J	F	M	A	M	J
J	A	S	O	N	D

Reverdin's Blue

Lycaeides argyrognomon

ID FACT FILE

WINGSPAN:
2.5–3.2 cm

DESCRIPTION:
Male deep blue
with narrow black
edges; female
dark brown,
usually with
some blue close
to body. Under-
side pale
brownish-grey
with black spots,
and row of
orange spots
near outer edges

**HIBERNATING
STAGE:**
Usually egg,
sometimes cater-
pillar

FLIGHT PERIOD:
Late spring and
mid-summer

**CATERPILLAR FOOD
PLANTS:**
Crown vetch
(*Coronilla varia*)
and related
plants

LOOKALIKES:
Idas Blue (p.57)
and Silver-
studded Blue
(p.64)

This butterfly is found mostly in central and
S Europe, from France eastwards, with one or
two isolated colonies further north. It prefers
open flowery fields and meadows up to around
1500 m. The caterpillar is green with white
and magenta stripes along the back and sides,
and is attended by ants. There are normally
two broods each year. This species is difficult
to tell apart from the Idas Blue without close
examination.

caterpillar

male

J	F	M	A	M	J
J	A	S	O	N	D

Idas Blue
Lycaeides idas

ID FACT FILE

WINGSPAN:
2.5–3 cm

DESCRIPTION:
Very similar to
Reverdin's Blue.
The most obvi-
ous difference is
on the under-
side, where the
black spots on
the inner edge of
the orange mark-
ings are arrow-
shaped in this
species (gently
curved in
Reverdin's Blue)

**HIBERNATING
STAGE:**
Caterpillar

FLIGHT PERIOD:
Early summer,
also late summer
in the south

**CATERPILLAR FOOD
PLANTS:**
Vetches (*Coronil-
la, Vicia*) and
related plants

LOOKALIKES:
Reverdin's Blue
(p.56) and Silver-
studded Blue
(p.64)

A commoner and far more widespread butterfly than the similar Reverdin's Blue, found
everywhere except the British Isles and the
southernmost parts of the continent. It is also
more likely to be found in the mountains, preferring meadows and heaths up to around
2500 m. The caterpillar is green with a darker
stripe along the back and white lines down the
sides. It is attended by ants, and spends the
winter within an ant nest.

female

left male
right female

J	F	M	A	M	J
J	A	S	O	N	D

Adonis Blue

Lysandra bellargus

ID FACT FILE

WINGSPAN:
2.7–3.2 cm

DESCRIPTION:
Male brilliant sky blue with fine black edges and broad white fringe; female dark brown with a row of orange crescents near the outer edge of each wing and blue close to body. In both sexes, underside pale brown with black spots and a row of orange crescents

HIBERNATING STAGE:
Caterpillar

FLIGHT PERIOD:
Late spring and mid- to late summer

CATERPILLAR FOOD PLANTS:
Horseshoe vetch (*Hippocrepis*) and related plants

A butterfly of chalk and limestone hills, commonly found throughout most of Europe except the far north. In the British Isles it is found only in S England in small, isolated colonies. It prefers open grassland on low hillsides but can be found up to around 2000 m. The caterpillar is clear deep green with yellow lines along the back and sides, and is attended at all times by ants. There are normally two broods each year.

male

female

J	F	M	A	M	J
J	A	S	O	N	D

Chalkhill Blue
Lysandra coridon

ID FACT FILE

WINGSPAN:
3–3.5 cm

DESCRIPTION:
Male silvery blue with black edges; female dark brown with orange and white spots on hindwings and some blue near body. In both sexes, underside pale brownish-grey with black spots. Many different forms

HIBERNATING STAGE:
Caterpillar

FLIGHT PERIOD:
Mid-summer

CATERPILLAR FOOD PLANTS:
Horseshoe vetch (*Hippocrepis*) and related plants

This extremely variable butterfly is found throughout most of Europe except Scandinavia and the extreme south. In the British Isles it is found only in S England. It is restricted to chalk and limestone hills up to around 2000 m, and prefers flowery fields and meadows. The caterpillar is green with yellow stripes along the back and sides, and normally feeds at night, attended by ants. The pupa, too, is usually guarded by ants.

male

female

Alcon Blue

Maculinea alcon

J	F	M	A	M	J
J	A	S	O	N	D

ID FACT FILE

WINGSPAN:
3–3.5 cm

DESCRIPTION:
Male blue with broad black edges, female dark greyish-brown with some blue near body and black spots on forewings. In both sexes, underside pale brown with black spots

HIBERNATING STAGE:
Caterpillar

FLIGHT PERIOD:
Early summer

CATERPILLAR FOOD PLANTS:
Gentians (*Gentiana*) in early stages; ant larvae later

LOOKALIKES:
Large Blue (p.61)

This butterfly is found mostly in central Europe, with a few isolated colonies in the south. It prefers grasslands and meadows in both damp and dry conditions up to around 2000 m. In its early stages the caterpillar is a dull green or reddish-brown, but this changes to pale creamy brown once it moves underground to feed within an ant nest. Pupation takes place inside the nest in the spring. There is a distinct subspecies, which is usually found at higher elevations.

female

male

Large Blue
Maculinea arion

J	F	M	A	M	J
J	A	S	O	N	D

ID FACT FILE

WINGSPAN:
2.8–3.8 cm

DESCRIPTION:
Male light blue with black edges and black spots on forewings; female similar but with more and larger spots and broader edges. In both sexes underside pale greyish-brown with black spots, which are larger on the forewings than they are on Alcon Blue

HIBERNATING STAGE:
Caterpillar

FLIGHT PERIOD:
Early summer

CATERPILLAR FOOD PLANTS:
Thyme (*Thymus*) in early stages, feeding on ant larvae when taken under-ground by ants

LOOKALIKES:
Alcon Blue (p.60)

This butterfly is fairly common throughout the greater part of Europe, except for the far north. In Spain it is found mainly in the central mountains, while in the British Isles it has become extinct in recent years, although attempts are being made to reintroduce it. It prefers rough grassland, wherever the food plant grows, in conjunction with suitable ant nests. The caterpillar is brownish-pink at first, changing to pale creamy brown when it moves underground.

female

male

LYCAENIDAE (BLUES, COPPERS AND HAIRSTREAKS)

J	F	M	A	M	J
J	A	S	O	N	D

Meleager's Blue
Meleageria daphnis

ID FACT FILE

WINGSPAN:
3–3.5 cm

DESCRIPTION:
Male brilliant
light blue with
narrow black
edges, female
darker blue,
black edges
broader. Hind-
wings of both
sexes slightly
scalloped, but
clearer in female.
Underside pale
brown – darker in
female – with
black spots

**HIBERNATING
STAGE:**
Caterpillar

FLIGHT PERIOD:
Early summer

**CATERPILLAR FOOD
PLANTS:**
Thyme (*Thymus*),
milk-vetches
(*Astragalus*) and
related plants

A fairly common butterfly in the warmer parts
of Europe, from the S France eastwards. It
likes sunny and flowery limestone hillsides
from lowlands up to around 1800 m. The
caterpillar is green with a darker line down the
back and yellowish stripes either side of this
and along the sides. It is attended by ants
throughout its life, and when fully grown in
the spring it pupates at ground level amongst
leaf-litter.

male underside

left male
right female

J	F	M	A	M	J
J	A	S	O	N	D

Baton Blue
Philotes baton

ID FACT FILE

WINGSPAN:
2–2.5cm

DESCRIPTION:
Male pale blue
with broad black
edges; female
plain dark brown,
sometimes with
blue near body.
In both sexes,
underside very
pale grey-brown
with black spots
and a row of light
orange spots
near edges of
hindwings

**HIBERNATING
STAGE:**
Caterpillar or
pupa

FLIGHT PERIOD:
Late spring and
late summer

**CATERPILLAR FOOD
PLANTS:**
Thyme (*Thymus*)

Although widely distributed throughout central
and S Europe, this butterfly is not especially
common. Further east it may be found as far
north as Finland. It likes flowery, open hillsides up to around 2000 m, wherever the food
plant grows. The caterpillars are bluish-green
with magenta and white stripes along the back
and sides, matching perfectly the flowers on
which it feeds. There are two broods each year,
but only one higher up in the mountains.

female underside

left male
right female

J	F	M	A	M	J
J	A	S	O	N	D

Silver-studded Blue
Plebejus argus

ID FACT FILE

WINGSPAN:
2–2.3 cm

DESCRIPTION:
Similar to Idas
and Reverdin's
Blues, but males
can be identified
easily by a short
spur on front
legs not present
in other species

**HIBERNATING
STAGE:**
Egg

FLIGHT PERIOD:
Late spring, also
late summer in
south

**CATERPILLAR FOOD
PLANTS:**
Various low-
growing plants
including bird's-
foot-trefoil
(*Lotus*), gorse
(*Ulex*) and ling
(*Calluna*)

LOOKALIKES:
Idas Blue (p.57)
and Reverdin's
Blue (p.56)

With the exception of the most northerly parts
of Scandinavia, this very common butterfly is
found throughout Europe. In the British Isles
it is found only in S England and N Wales. It
prefers sunny heaths and grasslands on chalk
hills up to around 2500 m. The caterpillar,
which may be variable shades of green, striped
along the back and sides in magenta and white,
feeds mainly on flowers and is always attended
by ants.

male

female

LYCAENIDAE (BLUES, COPPERS AND HAIRSTREAKS)

J	F	M	A	M	J
J	A	S	O	N	D

Turquoise Blue
Plebicula dorylas

This is very much a mountain butterfly, found mainly in central and S Europe, but with one or two isolated colonies further north. It prefers sunny and flowery meadows mainly between 1000 m and 2000 m. The caterpillar is very pale greenish-yellow with lighter spots in a line down the back. It is attended at all times by ants, and when fully grown pupates near ground level under a leaf of the food plant.

ID FACT FILE

WINGSPAN:
2.5–3 cm

DESCRIPTION:
Male bright sky blue with narrow black edges; female dark brown with orange crescents near edges of hindwings, some-times also on forewings. In both sexes, underside pale grey-brown with black spots and orange and white markings along outer edges

HIBERNATING STAGE:
Caterpillar

FLIGHT PERIOD:
Early and late summer

CATERPILLAR FOOD PLANTS:
Thyme (*Thymus*), kidney vetch (*Anthyllis*) and related plants

male

left male
right female

LYCAENIDAE (BLUES, COPPERS AND HAIRSTREAKS)

J	F	M	A	M	J
J	A	S	O	N	D

Common Blue
Polyommatus icarus

This is one of the commonest butterflies, as its name may suggest, and is found throughout Europe, preferring meadows and flowery hill-sides up to around 2500 m, although it is some-times seen in gardens. The caterpillar is green with a darker line down the back and yellowish stripes along the sides. Like many blues, they show a preference for flowers when feeding, and are normally attended by ants. Pupation takes place at ground level.

ID FACT FILE

WINGSPAN:
2.5–3 cm

DESCRIPTION:
Male light violet-blue, very finely edged with black; female dark brown, often with some blue close to the body and with orange crescents near the outer edges of all 4 wings. In both sexes, underside pale brownish-grey with blue near the body, marked with orange crescents near edges of hindwings, and black spots

HIBERNATING STAGE:
Caterpillar

FLIGHT PERIOD:
Mid-spring to late summer; 2 or 3 broods

CATERPILLAR FOOD PLANTS:
Bird's-foot-trefoil (*Lotus*), clover (*Trifolium*) and many other related plants

male

female

J	F	M	A	M	J
J	A	S	O	N	D

Chequered Blue
Scolitantides orion

ID FACT FILE

WINGSPAN:
2.2–2.8 cm

DESCRIPTION:
Male dark grey, almost black, marked with dull blue especially close to the body; female similar but darker with less blue. In both sexes, underside white with large black spots and a prominent band of orange on the hindwings

HIBERNATING STAGE:
Pupa

FLIGHT PERIOD:
Mid-summer, but in the south first brood is in late spring

CATERPILLAR FOOD PLANTS:
Stonecrops (*Sedum*)

This butterfly has an interesting distribution as it is found in two distinct areas of Europe: S Europe and S Scandinavia. In both areas it prefers rough, dry and stony south-facing slopes up to around 1800 m. There are two broods each year in the south, but only one in the north. The caterpillar is green, heavily marked with violet-magenta, and is always attended by ants. Pupation takes place on the food plant near the ground.

left male
right female

J	F	M	A	M	J
J	A	S	O	N	D

Lang's Short-tailed Blue
Syntarucus pirithous

ID FACT FILE

WINGSPAN:
2.2–2.5 cm

DESCRIPTION:
Male light violet-blue finely edged with black; 2 small black spots close to the short tail on the hindwings. Female similar but with much of the blue replaced by dark brown. In both sexes, underside marbled pattern of brown and white

HIBERNATING STAGE:
Caterpillar

FLIGHT PERIOD:
Early spring to late summer in several broods

CATERPILLAR FOOD PLANTS:
Bladder-senna (*Colutea*), broom (*Cytisus*) and related plants

LOOKALIKES:
Long-tailed Blue (p.55)

This little butterfly is fairly common throughout S Europe, preferring sunny, open waste ground, usually at low levels. It migrates regularly every summer – and this is normally the only time it is seen at high elevations – but it rarely flies very far north. The caterpillar is a pale yellowish-green with even paler and rather indistinct markings, and is normally attended by ants. Pupation takes place close to the ground.

left male
right female

LYCAENIDAE (BLUES, COPPERS AND HAIRSTREAKS)

J	F	M	A	M	J
J	A	S	O	N	D

Cranberry Blue
Vacciniina optilete

ID FACT FILE

WINGSPAN:
2.2–2.5 cm

DESCRIPTION:
Male dark violet-blue finely edged with black; female dark brown with some blue close to the body. In both sexes, underside dusky grey with black spots and a prominent reddish-orange spot on hind-wings

HIBERNATING STAGE:
Caterpillar

FLIGHT PERIOD:
Mid-summer

CATERPILLAR FOOD PLANTS:
Cranberry (*Vaccinium*) and related plants

This butterfly has a distribution that takes in the whole of the NE part of Europe, from the central Alps to Scandinavia and eastwards. It prefers peat moorlands and south-facing mountain slopes up to around 2500 m. Living in colder climates, it produces only one brood each year. The caterpillar is clear green with a pink and white stripe along the sides, and when fully grown it pupates under a leaf of the food plant.

caterpillar

male

J	F	M	A	M	J
J	A	S	O	N	D

Purple-shot Copper
Heodes alciphron

ID FACT FILE

WINGSPAN:
3–3.8 cm

DESCRIPTION:
Male shining reddish-orange mostly overlaid with violet-purple and some dark spots; female dark brown with black spots and row of orange spots on hindwings. In both sexes, underside has black spots larger than Purple-edged Copper

HIBERNATING STAGE:
Caterpillar

FLIGHT PERIOD:
Early summer

CATERPILLAR FOOD PLANTS:
Dock (*Rumex*)

LOOKALIKES:
Purple-edged Copper (p.74)

This butterfly is found across most of Europe, but is absent from Scandinavia, the British Isles and the northernmost parts of France and Belgium. It prefers lowland meadows and fields up to around 1000 m, but there is a distinct subspecies which is only found on grassy mountain slopes between 1500 m and 2000 m. The caterpillar is green with darker stripes down the back and sides, and is usually attended by ants. Unusually for a butterfly, pupation takes place underground.

male

female

J	F	M	A	M	J
J	A	S	O	N	D

Sooty Copper
Heodes tityrus

ID FACT FILE

WINGSPAN:
2.3–3 cm

DESCRIPTION:
Male dark greyish-brown with black spots and a faint row of orange crescents on hindwings; female similar but with orange markings extended to forewings. In both sexes, underside pale brownish-grey with black spots

HIBERNATING STAGE:
Caterpillar

FLIGHT PERIOD:
Mid-spring and late summer

CATERPILLAR FOOD PLANTS:
Dock (*Rumex*)

This butterfly is found throughout most of central and S Europe but not the far north or the British Isles. In Spain it occurs only in very isolated colonies and everywhere else it is rather local, preferring flowery meadows and hillsides, usually in lowland country, although it can be found up to around 2000 m. There are two broods each year. The caterpillar is bright green with white spots, and is always attended by ants. Pupation takes place at ground level amongst leaf-litter.

female

male

LYCAENIDAE (BLUES, COPPERS AND HAIRSTREAKS)

J	F	M	A	M	J
J	A	S	O	N	D

Scarce Copper
Heodes virgaureae

ID FACT FILE

WINGSPAN:
2.7–3.2 cm

DESCRIPTION:
Male shining
coppery-orange
with black edges;
female paler
orange with large
black spots and
narrower black
edges. In both
sexes, underside
light yellowish-
brown with black
and white spots

**HIBERNATING
STAGE:**
Caterpillar

FLIGHT PERIOD:
Mid-summer

**CATERPILLAR FOOD
PLANTS:**
Dock (*Rumex*)

A very widespread butterfly, locally common
right across Europe to S Scandinavia, but not
found in the British Isles, N France or S Italy.
It prefers flowery meadows and forest clearings, especially near streams, up to around
2000 m. The caterpillar is green with a few
whitish spots and is normally attended by ants.
When fully grown it pupates under a leaf on
the food plant.

male

female

Small Copper
Lycaena phlaeas

J	F	M	A	M	J
J	A	S	O	N	D

ID FACT FILE

WINGSPAN:
2.2–2.7 cm

DESCRIPTION:
Forewings
shining coppery-
orange with dark
brown edges and
black spots;
hindwings dark
brown with cop-
pery band close
to outer edges.
Underside pale
grey-brown with
black spots.
Sexes alike

HIBERNATING STAGE:
Caterpillar

FLIGHT PERIOD:
Early spring to
early autumn

CATERPILLAR FOOD PLANTS:
Dock and sorrel
(*Rumex*), and
knotgrass
(*Polygonum*)

caterpillar

This very common butterfly is found throughout Europe, and prefers sunny meadows and
forest clearings up to around 2000 m. Males
are extremely territorial, chasing any intruders
away, even birds! There are normally two,
sometimes three broods each year, third
generation adults are often much smaller. The
caterpillar is green, sometimes with a dark pink
stripe down the back and sides, and is attended
by ants. It usually pupates under a leaf of the
food plant.

J	F	M	A	M	J
J	A	S	O	N	D

Purple-edged Copper
Palaeochrysophanus hippothoe

ID FACT FILE

WINGSPAN:
2.8–3.5 cm

DESCRIPTION:
Male red-gold with purple iridescence spreading from black borders; female dark brown with some orange on forewings and coppery band near edges of hindwings. In both sexes, underside greyish-brown with black spots

HIBERNATING STAGE:
Caterpillar

FLIGHT PERIOD:
Early summer

CATERPILLAR FOOD PLANTS:
Dock (*Rumex*) and knotgrass (*Polygonum*)

LOOKALIKES:
Purple-shot Copper (p.70)

A rather local butterfly found throughout most of Europe but more so in the east. Further west towards Spain colonies become far more isolated, and it is absent from the British Isles. It prefers damp meadows and bogs up to around 2000 m, and drainage of these wetland areas may be why this species is declining in numbers. The caterpillar is green with a darker line down the back and white lines along the sides.

male

female

LYCAENIDAE (BLUES, COPPERS AND HAIRSTREAKS)

J	F	M	A	M	J
J	A	S	O	N	D

Green Hairstreak
Callophrys rubi

ID FACT FILE

WINGSPAN:
2.4–2.8 cm

DESCRIPTION:
Plain greyish-brown; underside green with several white spots in a row on the hindwings

HIBERNATING STAGE:
Pupa

FLIGHT PERIOD:
Spring to early summer, depending on locality

CATERPILLAR FOOD PLANTS:
Many low-growing plants including gorse (*Ulex*), ling (*Calluna*) and bramble (*Rubus*)

A common butterfly found throughout most of Europe and tolerating a wide range of situations, from wet or dry heaths to open woodland up to around 2100 m. The caterpillar is green with a darker stripe down the back and yellowish stripes along the sides. It eats mainly flowers and young fruits or seed-pods, and when fully grown it pupates at ground level near the food plant. The pupa can make an audible noise.

caterpillar

Sloe Hairstreak
Nordmannia acaciae

ID FACT FILE

WINGSPAN:
2.3–2.8 cm

DESCRIPTION:
Dark brown with small orange spot near short tail. Underside brownish-grey with white line across each wing (female has only partial line across hindwings) and orange band near edge of hindwings

HIBERNATING STAGE:
Caterpillar

FLIGHT PERIOD:
Early summer

CATERPILLAR FOOD PLANTS:
Sloe (*Prunus*)

LOOKALIKES:
Ilex Hairstreak (p.77)

This butterfly is found right across central and S Europe with the exception of S Spain. It prefers rough, open hillsides, wherever the food plant grows, up to around 1800 m. Eggs are normally covered by a few hairs from the female, presumably in an attempt to stop parasitic flies or wasps from finding them. The caterpillar is pale green with lighter stripes along the back and sides and when fully grown, pupates at ground level.

left male
right female

J	F	M	A	M	J
J	A	S	O	N	D

Ilex Hairstreak

Nordmannia ilicis

ID FACT FILE

WINGSPAN:
2.6–3 cm

DESCRIPTION:
Male dark brown, sometimes with orange patch on forewings, female larger and paler with more orange. In both sexes, underside grey-ish-brown with a broken white line across each wing and red spots near hindwing edges

HIBERNATING STAGE:
Egg

FLIGHT PERIOD:
Early summer

CATERPILLAR FOOD PLANTS:
Oak (*Quercus*)

LOOKALIKES:
Sloe Hairstreak (p.76)

This butterfly can be found throughout most of Europe except S Spain, the British Isles and N Scandinavia. It prefers open woodland and rough ground, usually on hillsides up to around 1800 m. The caterpillar is pale green with a darker line down the back and sides, and is attended by ants. It feeds on low-growing bushy young plants, and when fully grown pupates on top of a leaf, when it looks like a bird-dropping.

left male
right female

LYCAENIDAE (BLUES, COPPERS AND HAIRSTREAKS)

J	F	M	A	M	J
J	A	S	O	N	D

Purple Hairstreak
Quercusia quercus

ID FACT FILE

WINGSPAN:
3–3.8 cm

DESCRIPTION:
Female dark
brown with bright
violet-blue patch
on forewings;
male also dark
brown almost
completely
overlaid with a
dull violet sheen.
In both sexes,
underside mid-
grey with a white
line across each
wing and 2
orange spots on
the hindwings
close to very
short tails

**HIBERNATING
STAGE:**
Egg

FLIGHT PERIOD:
Mid-summer

**CATERPILLAR FOOD
PLANTS:**
Oak (*Quercus*),
sometimes ash
(*Fraxinus*)

A woodland butterfly, found in oak forests
throughout most of Europe, except Scotland
and N Scandinavia, up to around 2000 m. The
adults are not seen very often because they
spend most of their time flying high up around
tree tops and do not come down to flowers,
feeding instead on sticky honey-dew from
aphids. The caterpillar is reddish-brown with a
darker line down the back, bordered with paler
triangular markings.

male

female

Black Hairstreak
Strymondia pruni

J	F	M	A	M	J
J	A	S	O	N	D

ID FACT FILE

WINGSPAN:
2.8–3.5 cm

DESCRIPTION:
Male dark brown with orange spots on hind-wings close to the tail; female similar but with some orange on the forewings. In both sexes, underside mid-brown with a wide band of orange bordered by black spots, and a thin white line across each wing

HIBERNATING STAGE:
Egg

FLIGHT PERIOD:
Early summer

CATERPILLAR FOOD PLANTS:
Sloe (*Prunus*) and related trees

LOOKALIKES:
White-letter Hair-streak (p.81)

This is a rather local butterfly found mainly in central and E Europe. In the British Isles it is very rare, confined to a few small areas in central England. It is a lowland butterfly, preferring woodland and hedgerows below 1,000 m, wherever the food plant grows. The caterpillar is pale green, striped down the back with magenta and white. The pupa looks very much like a bird-dropping and is formed on top of a leaf.

caterpillar

LYCAENIDAE (BLUES, COPPERS AND HAIRSTREAKS)

J	F	M	A	M	J
J	A	S	O	N	D

Blue-spot Hairstreak
Strymondia spini

ID FACT FILE

WINGSPAN:
2.8–3.2 cm

DESCRIPTION:
Male dark brown
with small
orange spots
near the tail on
hindwings;
female similar
but larger and
paler. In both
sexes, underside
mid-brown with
white line across
each wing; hind-
wings marked
with short orange
band and promi-
nent blue spot

**HIBERNATING
STAGE:**
Egg

FLIGHT PERIOD:
Early summer

**CATERPILLAR FOOD
PLANTS:**
Buckthorn
(*Rhamnus*) and
sloe (*Prunus*)

This butterfly is commonly found throughout
central and S Europe, with the exception of
the southern tip of Italy and the Mediterranean islands. It prefers dry, open woodland
and shrubby hillsides up to around 2000 m,
wherever the food plant grows. The caterpillar
is pale green with yellowish stripes down the
back and sides, and is attended by ants. The
pale brown pupa is hidden under a leaf on the
food plant.

caterpillar

| J | F | M | A | M | J |
| J | A | S | O | N | D |

White-letter Hairstreak

Strymondia w-album

ID FACT FILE

WINGSPAN:
2.7–3.2 cm

DESCRIPTION:
Male plain dark brown; female slightly paler with orange spot near tails. In both sexes, underside mid-brown with white line across each wing – forming clear 'W' on hindwings – and reddish-orange band near edge of hindwings

HIBERNATING STAGE:
Egg

FLIGHT PERIOD:
Early summer

CATERPILLAR FOOD PLANTS:
Elm (*Ulmus*)

LOOKALIKES:
Black Hairstreak (p.79)

This butterfly is widespread throughout central and S Europe, including southern parts of England and Scandinavia. In Spain it is found only in the north in small colonies, and it is very rare in the Netherlands. It prefers woodland clearings and edges, and also small copses, wherever elm trees grow; it is easily attracted to bramble flowers. The caterpillar feeds on elm flowers at first, moving to leaves later, and is attended by ants.

caterpillar

LYCAENIDAE (BLUES, COPPERS AND HAIRSTREAKS)

J	F	M	A	M	J
J	A	S	O	N	D

Brown Hairstreak
Thecla betulae

ID FACT FILE

WINGSPAN:
3.4–3.8 cm

DESCRIPTION:
Male dark brown with a small faint patch on forewings and orange spots on the tails; female similar but with large bright orange patch on forewings. In both sexes, underside bright yellow-brown with orange edges and white lines across each wing

HIBERNATING STAGE:
Egg

FLIGHT PERIOD:
Mid-summer

CATERPILLAR FOOD PLANTS:
Sloe (*Prunus*) and related shrubs

This is a fairly common butterfly through much of Europe except the far north and the extreme south. It is a lowland butterfly, preferring open woodland and hedgerows, where it will normally fly high up in the tree tops. Like the Purple Hairstreak, it is not attracted to flowers, feeding instead on sweet and sticky honey-dew from aphids. The well-hidden caterpillar is green with yellow markings to look like a leaf.

male

female

RIODINIDAE (METALMARKS)

Duke of Burgundy Fritillary

Hamearis lucina

J	F	M	A	M	J
J	A	S	O	N	D

ID FACT FILE

WINGSPAN:
2.8–3.4 cm

DESCRIPTION:
Dark brown with light orange-brown spots. Underside orange-brown with dark spots on forewings, white spots on hindwings. Female brighter

HIBERNATING STAGE:
Pupa

FLIGHT PERIOD:
Late spring and late summer, late spring only in the north

CATERPILLAR FOOD PLANTS:
Cowslip and primrose (*Primula*)

This butterfly is locally fairly common throughout most of central and S Europe, although in some places it is becoming rarer. It is also found in some parts of England, mainly in the south, and S Scandinavia, but it is absent from S Spain. It prefers open woodland, usually in lowland areas. The caterpillar is pale brown in colour marked with darker lines and spots, and always stays underneath a leaf, which is where it will later pupate.

female

male

J	F	M	A	M	J
J	A	S	O	N	D

Small Tortoiseshell
Aglais urticae

ID FACT FILE

WINGSPAN:
4.5–5 cm

DESCRIPTION:
Orange-red
ground colour
with black mark-
ings, edged
black with blue
crescents.
Underside dark,
almost black.
Sexes alike

**HIBERNATING
STAGE:**
Adult

FLIGHT PERIOD:
Spring, and early
summer to
autumn

**CATERPILLAR FOOD
PLANTS:**
Nettle (*Urtica*)

LOOKALIKES:
Large Tortoise-
shell (p.118)

Found throughout Europe, this is probably one
of the most popular butterflies seen in gardens,
where they favour *Buddleia* and *Sedum* flowers
at the height of summer. They are also often
found indoors in the winter when a warm spell
might rouse them from hibernation. Males are
territorial. There are two broods each year
except in the far north. Caterpillars live in communal webs when young, for protection against
predators. Shortly before pupating, they will
separate and feed alone.

caterpillars

| J | F | M | A | M | J |
| J | A | S | O | N | D |

Lesser Purple Emperor
Apatura ilia

ID FACT FILE

WINGSPAN:
6.4–7 cm

DESCRIPTION:
Very variable but
mainly dark
brown with white
bands. Male has
a blue sheen. In
both sexes,
underside paler,
less white. Easily
recognised by
the small orange
circle on upper
forewings

**HIBERNATING
STAGE:**
Caterpillar

FLIGHT PERIOD:
Late spring and
late summer

**CATERPILLAR FOOD
PLANTS:**
Poplar (*Populus*)
and willow (*Salix*)

LOOKALIKES:
Purple Emperor
(p.86)

This is a lowland butterfly found in damp,
open woodland throughout central and parts of
S Europe. It spends most of its time flying
round tree tops, coming down only to feed
from damp ground, tree-sap and carrion.
There are usually two broods each year, but
may only be one further north. The pale green
caterpillar looks rather slug-like and has two
yellow horns on its head and a series of yellowish diagonal stripes along the sides. The leaf-
like pupa is suspended from under a leaf.

male

female

Purple Emperor
Apatura iris

J	F	M	A	M	J
J	A	S	O	N	D

ID FACT FILE

WINGSPAN:
6.2–7.5 cm

DESCRIPTION:
Dark brown with white bands and spots. Male has blue sheen. Underside similar but paler. Female much larger

HIBERNATING STAGE:
Caterpillar

FLIGHT PERIOD:
Mid-summer

CATERPILLAR FOOD PLANTS:
Sallow and willow (*Salix*)

LOOKALIKES:
Lesser Purple Emperor (p.85)

This butterfly is found throughout the lowlands of central and E Europe; in the British Isles it is restricted to S England. It is a woodland species that normally flies high in the trees, coming down only to feed from carrion, dung and tree-sap. The slug-like caterpillar is very similar to that of the Lesser Purple Emperor, but the horns on the head are tipped with red. The pupa is amazingly leaf-like, and formed under a leaf.

male

female

NYMPHALIDAE (BRUSH-FOOTED BUTTERFLIES)

J	F	M	A	M	J
J	A	S	O	N	D

Map Butterfly
Araschnia levana

This little butterfly is common throughout the lowlands of central and E Europe, preferring open woodland and forest edges. There are two broods each year, and the adults from the spring generation are remarkably different from those of the summer. Eggs are laid in strings under leaves, and the young caterpillars live in groups, separating when nearly fully grown. They are mainly black with rows of black or brown branching spines.

ID FACT FILE

WINGSPAN:
3.2–4 cm

DESCRIPTION:
First generation, light orange-brown with dark brown and white spots; second, dark brown with white bands. Underside reddish-brown with white bands and yellowish edges. Sexes alike

HIBERNATING STAGE:
Pupa

FLIGHT PERIOD:
Late spring and late summer

CATERPILLAR FOOD PLANTS:
Nettle (*Urtica*)

underside of 2nd brood

left male 1st brood
right male 2nd brood

NYMPHALIDAE (BRUSH-FOOTED BUTTERFLIES)

J	F	M	A	M	J
J	A	S	O	N	D

High Brown Fritillary
Argynnis adippe

ID FACT FILE

WINGSPAN:
5–6.2 cm

DESCRIPTION:
Light orange-brown with black spots. Underside yellowish-brown, with black spots on forewings and silver spots on hindwings. Sexes alike

HIBERNATING STAGE:
Egg

FLIGHT PERIOD:
Early summer

CATERPILLAR FOOD PLANTS:
Violet (*Viola*)

LOOKALIKES:
Niobe Fritillary (p.91) and Dark Green Fritillary (p.89)

A fairly common butterfly found throughout Europe except N Scandinavia, Scotland and Ireland. This is a very variable species with many named forms. It prefers open woodland and forest edges up to around 2500 m. It is a fast flier, fond of visiting flowers and also of drinking from damp ground. When fully grown the caterpillar will usually draw a few leaves of the food plant together to make a shelter before pupating.

caterpillar

NYMPHALIDAE (BRUSH-FOOTED BUTTERFLIES)

J	F	M	A	M	J
J	A	S	O	N	D

Dark Green Fritillary
Argynnis aglaja

ID FACT FILE

WINGSPAN:
4.8–5.5 cm

DESCRIPTION:
Very similar to
High Brown
Fritillary, but with
olive-green mark-
ings on hindwing
undersides. Also
silver spots
closest to body
widely separated.
Sexes alike

HIBERNATING STAGE:
Caterpillar

FLIGHT PERIOD:
Early summer

CATERPILLAR FOOD PLANTS:
Violet (*Viola*)

LOOKALIKES:
High Brown Fritil-
lary (p.88) and
Niobe Fritillary
(p.91)

This butterfly is found throughout Europe,
although in some areas it may be only locally
common. It prefers meadows, heaths and open
woodland up to around 3000 m. The caterpillar
hatches from its egg in August, and, after eating the eggshell, goes straight in to hibernation, eating nothing more until the first warm
days of spring. When fully grown it will pull a
few leaves together to make a shelter in which
it can pupate.

caterpillar

NYMPHALIDAE (BRUSH-FOOTED BUTTERFLIES)

J	F	M	A	M	J
J	A	S	O	N	D

Queen of Spain Fritillary
Argynnis lathonia

ID FACT FILE

WINGSPAN:
3.8–5 cm

DESCRIPTION:
Bright orange-brown with black spots. Underside slightly paler, with black spots on forewings, hindwings with very large silver spots. Sexes alike

HIBERNATING STAGE:
Egg, caterpillar, pupa or adult, depending on locality

FLIGHT PERIOD:
Early spring to early autumn

CATERPILLAR FOOD PLANTS:
Violet (*Viola*)

A common butterfly in S Europe, but also a well-known migrant that spreads to most of the rest of the continent every summer, reaching as far north as S Scandinavia. It is, however, a very rare visitor to the British Isles. It prefers meadows and heaths up to around 2500 m, and in the south there may be two or three broods each year. The fully grown caterpillar pupates under a leaf on the food plant.

caterpillar

NYMPHALIDAE (BRUSH-FOOTED BUTTERFLIES)

| J | F | M | A | M | J |
| J | A | S | O | N | D |

Niobe Fritillary
Argynnis niobe

ID FACT FILE

WINGSPAN:
4.6–5.5 cm

DESCRIPTION:
Very similar to,
but smaller than,
High Brown
Fritillary, but
veins on under-
side hindwings
picked out in
black. Silver
spots may be
absent

**HIBERNATING
STAGE:**
Caterpillar

FLIGHT PERIOD:
Early summer

**CATERPILLAR FOOD
PLANTS:**
Violet (*Viola*),
sometimes plan-
tain (*Plantago*)

LOOKALIKES:
High Brown
Fritillary (p.88)
and Dark Green
Fritillary (p.89)

This butterfly is commonly found throughout
Europe, but is absent from N Scandinavia and
the British Isles. It prefers flowery meadows
and woodland edges up to around 2500 m.
There are two main forms of this butterfly, the
commonest having no silver spots on the
underside, but in some areas – such as central
France – the type species is commoner. Newly
hatched caterpillars eat no food until the following spring, and when they are fully grown,
pupate under a leaf.

caterpillar

NYMPHALIDAE (BRUSH-FOOTED BUTTERFLIES)

J	F	M	A	M	J
J	A	S	O	N	D

Silver-washed Fritillary
Argynnis paphia

ID FACT FILE

WINGSPAN:
5.5–7cm

DESCRIPTION:
Bright orange-brown with black spots and lines. Underside forewings similar, hindwings olive-green with silver streaks. Female darker

HIBERNATING STAGE:
Caterpillar

FLIGHT PERIOD:
Early to mid-summer

CATERPILLAR FOOD PLANTS:
Violet (*Viola*)

LOOKALIKES:
Cardinal (p.119)

This is a fairly common butterfly of open woodland and forest, found throughout Europe except N Scandinavia and S Spain. In the British Isles it is confined to southern parts of England and Wales, and also Ireland. Eggs are laid in mid-summer on tree trunks, and newly hatched caterpillars eat nothing more than their eggshells until the following spring. They are black with two yellow lines down the back and rows of branched brown spines.

male

female

J	F	M	A	M	J
J	A	S	O	N	D

Cranberry Fritillary
Boloria aquilonaris

ID FACT FILE

WINGSPAN:
3.2–3.5 cm

DESCRIPTION:
Light orange-brown with black spots. Underside paler with reddish-brown markings and yellowish and black spots. Female darker, more heavily marked

HIBERNATING STAGE:
Caterpillar

FLIGHT PERIOD:
Early summer

CATERPILLAR FOOD PLANTS:
Cranberry (*Vaccinium*)

Although found in the lowlands, this is mainly a mountain butterfly, common throughout central and NE Europe. It prefers boggy and swampy places, up to around 2000 m. In the coldest areas the life-cycle may take two years to complete, the caterpillar hibernating through two winters. During hibernation it will sometimes shelter inside a stem of the food plant. It is black with two whitish lines down the back and rows of yellow branching spines.

mating pair

caterpillar

NYMPHALIDAE (BRUSH-FOOTED BUTTERFLIES)

J	F	M	A	M	J
J	A	S	O	N	D

Violet Fritillary
Boloria dia

ID FACT FILE

WINGSPAN:
3–3.4 cm

DESCRIPTION:
Light orange-brown with black spots. Underside forewings similar but paler, hind-wings purple-brown with white spots. Sexes alike

HIBERNATING STAGE:
Caterpillar

FLIGHT PERIOD:
Mid-spring to early autumn

CATERPILLAR FOOD PLANTS:
Violet (*Viola*) and bramble (*Rubus*)

One of the smallest of all the fritillaries, fairly common throughout most of central and E Europe but very local further south. It prefers open woodland, forest edges and meadows on low hillsides, no higher than 1000 m. There may be 2 or 3 broods each year, which often overlap slightly so that the butterfly seems to be on the wing continuously from spring right through to autumn.

caterpillar

NYMPHALIDAE (BRUSH-FOOTED BUTTERFLIES)

J	F	M	A	M	J
J	A	S	O	N	D

Pearl-bordered Fritillary

Boloria euphrosyne

ID FACT FILE

WINGSPAN:
3.8–4.6 cm

DESCRIPTION:
Light orange-brown with black spots. Underside similar but paler, forewings with black spots; hindwings with reddish-brown and silver spots. Sexes alike

HIBERNATING STAGE:
Caterpillar

FLIGHT PERIOD:
Mid- to late spring and mid-summer

CATERPILLAR FOOD PLANTS:
Violet (*Viola*)

LOOKALIKES:
Small Pearl-bordered Fritillary (p.96)

This butterfly is fairly common throughout Europe, but it is absent from S Spain, and in Ireland it is restricted to few localised colonies in the west. It prefers open woodland, forest edges, meadows and heaths up to around 2000 m. There is normally only 1 brood each year, but in the warmer south there may be 2. The caterpillar spends the winter in a shelter made from rolling a leaf of the food plant.

caterpillar

NYMPHALIDAE (BRUSH-FOOTED BUTTERFLIES)

Small Pearl-bordered Fritillary
Boloria selene

J	F	M	A	M	J
J	A	S	O	N	D

ID FACT FILE

WINGSPAN:
3.6–4.2 cm

DESCRIPTION:
Very similar to
Pearl-bordered
Fritillary, but
brown spots on
underside hind-
wing are darker;
also more silver
spots near body.
Sexes alike

**HIBERNATING
STAGE:**
Caterpillar

FLIGHT PERIOD:
Early summer in
the north, mid-
spring and
mid-summer in
the south

**CATERPILLAR FOOD
PLANTS:**
Violet (*Viola*)

LOOKALIKES:
Pearl-bordered
Fritillary (p.95)

This butterfly is fairly common everywhere in
northern, central and some parts of S Europe,
but is absent from Ireland. It prefers open
woodland, although in mountain areas it also
flies in moorland and heaths up to around
2000 m. There is normally only one brood each
year in the north, two in the south. The caterpillar shelters in a rolled-up leaf during the
winter, and when fully grown pupates under a
leaf of the food plant.

caterpillar

NYMPHALIDAE (BRUSH-FOOTED BUTTERFLIES)

J	F	M	A	M	J
J	A	S	O	N	D

Thor's Fritillary
Boloria thore

ID FACT FILE

WINGSPAN:
4–4.8 cm

DESCRIPTION:
Variable orange-
brown with black
markings, very
heavy in the
south. Underside
brown with yellow
and white spots,
all very pale in
the north.
Female usually
larger

**HIBERNATING
STAGE:**
Caterpillar

FLIGHT PERIOD:
Early to
mid-summer

**CATERPILLAR FOOD
PLANTS:**
Violet (*Viola*)

This variable butterfly can be found in three
separate parts of Europe: the Alps, S Finland
and N Scandinavia. In Scandinavia adults are
very pale,and can be found in hilly areas close
to sea level. Elsewhere they are usually to be
seen above 1000 m up to around 2000 m. They
generally prefer light woodland. Caterpillars
must usually hibernate through two winters
before they can finally pupate under a
suitable leaf.

underside of northern race

caterpillar

J	F	M	A	M	J
J	A	S	O	N	D

Titania's Fritillary
Boloria titania

ID FACT FILE

WINGSPAN:
4.4–4.8 cm

DESCRIPTION:
Bright orange-brown with black markings. Underside hindwing marbled brown and cream with black spots. Female larger and paler

HIBERNATING STAGE:
Caterpillar

FLIGHT PERIOD:
Early to mid-summer

CATERPILLAR FOOD PLANTS:
Violets (*Viola*)

This butterfly can be found mainly east of the Baltic Sea into Russia, and also in small scattered colonies in the Alps, particularly Switzerland and N Italy. It prefers lightly wooded areas and the edges of forest clearings, usually above 1000 m up to around 2000 m. Adults living in the Alps have a definite purplish tint on the underside of the hindwings. The fully grown caterpillar usually pupates under a leaf of the food plant.

caterpillar

J	F	M	A	M	J
J	A	S	O	N	D

Marbled Fritillary
Brenthis daphne

ID FACT FILE

WINGSPAN:
4.2–5.2 cm

DESCRIPTION:
Light orange-brown with black spots. Underside forewings similar, underside hindwings marbled orange-brown and pale purple-brown with band of yellowish spots. Female similar but paler

HIBERNATING STAGE:
Caterpillar

FLIGHT PERIOD:
Early summer

CATERPILLAR FOOD PLANTS:
Violet (*Viola*) and bramble (*Rubus*)

LOOKALIKES:
Lesser Marbled Fritillary (p.100)

This is a fairly common butterfly throughout most of S Europe, where it prefers dry, sunny fields and meadows with plenty of flowers. It can be seen up to around 1500 m, but will normally keep to the warmer lowlands, and is very fond of bramble blossoms. The caterpillar is black with narrow white lines along the back and sides, and yellowish branching spines. When fully grown it pupates under a leaf of the food plant.

caterpillar

NYMPHALIDAE (BRUSH-FOOTED BUTTERFLIES)

Lesser Marbled Fritillary
Brenthis ino

J	F	M	A	M	J
J	A	S	O	N	D

ID FACT FILE

WINGSPAN:
3.4–4 cm

DESCRIPTION:
Very similar to
Marbled Fritillary,
but underside
hindwings have a
yellowish spot
near body

**HIBERNATING
STAGE:**
Caterpillar

FLIGHT PERIOD:
Early summer

**CATERPILLAR FOOD
PLANTS:**
Meadowsweet
(*Filipendula*),
goat's-beard
(*Aruncus*) and
related plants

LOOKALIKES:
Marbled Fritillary
(p.99)

This butterfly is common in local, scattered
colonies throughout most of northern and central Europe, except the British Isles, with just a
few colonies further south. It prefers marshes,
peat bogs and damp, open woodland, up to
around 1500 m, and is especially attracted to
bramble and thistle flowers. The caterpillar
feeds at night, spending the day around the
base of the food plant, and when fully grown
pupates under a leaf.

caterpillar

J	F	M	A	M	J
J	A	S	O	N	D

Two-tailed Pasha
Charaxes jasius

ID FACT FILE

WINGSPAN:
7.6–8.5 cm

DESCRIPTION:
Rich dark brown with wide yellow borders, double-tailed hindwings edged black. Underside multi-coloured pattern of spots and stripes with broad white band through the middle. Female larger

HIBERNATING STAGE:
Caterpillar

FLIGHT PERIOD:
Late spring and late summer

CATERPILLAR FOOD PLANTS:
Strawberry tree (*Arbutus*)

This distinctive butterfly is locally common in the coastal areas around the Mediterranean islands, also Portugal. It is a powerful, fast-flying species, spending most of the time high in the trees in lowland areas, coming down only to feed from rotten fruit. There are two broods each year, and eggs are usually laid quite low down on the food plant. When fully grown the caterpillar pupates under a leaf, the pupa looking very leaf-like.

caterpillar

NYMPHALIDAE (BRUSH-FOOTED BUTTERFLIES)

J	F	M	A	M	J
J	A	S	O	N	D

Painted Lady
Cynthia cardui

ID FACT FILE

WINGSPAN:
5.4–5.8 cm

DESCRIPTION:
Pale pinkish-brown with black spots, also white spots on forewings. Underside marbled pale and mid-brown with a row of blue eye-like spots on hind-wings. Sexes alike

HIBERNATING STAGE:
Adult, but only in extreme south

FLIGHT PERIOD:
Mid-spring to late autumn

CATERPILLAR FOOD PLANTS:
Thistle (*Carduus*) and nettle (*Urtica*)

This is not a true resident in Europe, as it migrates from Africa every year and is unable to survive the winter anywhere else except, perhaps, in the extreme south. However, it is a common sight everywhere during the summer, even in parks and gardens, up to around 2500 m. Migrants produce one, sometimes two broods each year. The young caterpillar usually makes a shelter out of one or two leaves, but will often stop doing this when much larger. It pupates inside a similar shelter.

caterpillar

NYMPHALIDAE (BRUSH-FOOTED BUTTERFLIES)

J	F	M	A	M	J
J	A	S	O	N	D

Marsh Fritillary
Eurodryas aurinia

ID FACT FILE

WINGSPAN:
3.5–4.6 cm

DESCRIPTION:
Pale yellowish-brown with orange-brown markings and dark brown spots. Underside light orange-brown with yellowish spots. Female larger and paler

HIBERNATING STAGE:
Caterpillar

FLIGHT PERIOD:
Late spring

CATERPILLAR FOOD PLANTS:
Scabious (*Scabiosa*) and plantain (*Plantago*)

This little butterfly is fairly common throughout most of Europe, although it is absent from N Scandinavia, and more local in Italy and the British Isles. It likes open spaces in both damp and dry conditions, such as bogs, moorland and meadows up to around 2200 m. The caterpillars are black with a pale stripe along each side and rows of branched spines. They live in groups, making a communal web for shelter through the winter, separating only when they are nearly fully grown.

female

male

NYMPHALIDAE (BRUSH-FOOTED BUTTERFLIES)

J	F	M	A	M	J
J	A	S	O	N	D

Peacock
Inachis io

ID FACT FILE

WINGSPAN:
5.4–5.8 cm

DESCRIPTION:
Dark reddish-brown with black and yellow markings and a large lilac-blue eye-like spot on each wing. Underside mostly black. Sexes alike

HIBERNATING STAGE:
Adult

FLIGHT PERIOD:
Mid-summer to early autumn and early to mid-spring

CATERPILLAR FOOD PLANTS:
Nettle (*Urtica*)

This very common butterfly is found throughout Europe except N Scotland and N Scandinavia. It can be seen anywhere there is a good supply of suitable flowers, especially parks and gardens, up to around 2000 m. The caterpillars live in groups when young, separating when nearly fully grown, and will often wander some distance from the food plant before pupating. Adults will often enter houses in the search for somewhere to pass the winter.

caterpillar

NYMPHALIDAE (BRUSH-FOOTED BUTTERFLIES)

| J | F | M | A | M | J |
| J | A | S | O | N | D |

White Admiral
Ladoga camilla

ID FACT FILE

WINGSPAN:
5.2–6 cm

DESCRIPTION:
Dark brown with a white band through the middle of each wing. Underside pattern similar but dark brown replaced by grey and tan. Sexes alike

HIBERNATING STAGE:
Caterpillar

FLIGHT PERIOD:
Early summer

CATERPILLAR FOOD PLANTS:
Honeysuckle (*Lonicera*)

LOOKALIKES:
Southern White Admiral (p.107)

This butterfly is found mainly throughout central and E Europe and just a few places further south. In the British Isles it is found only in S England. It is a woodland butterfly, preferring damp places up to around 1500 m, and is very attracted to bramble flowers. When very small, the brown caterpillar folds a leaf over and spends the winter sheltering inside. Only after hibernation in spring does it change to green.

caterpillar

NYMPHALIDAE (BRUSH-FOOTED BUTTERFLIES)

J	F	M	A	M	J
J	A	S	O	N	D

Poplar Admiral
Limenitis populi

ID FACT FILE

WINGSPAN:
7–8 cm

DESCRIPTION:
Dark brown with
whitish spots
and a row of
orange-brown
spots near edges
of hindwings.
Underside
orange-brown
and grey with
white spots.
Sexes alike

**HIBERNATING
STAGE:**
Caterpillar

FLIGHT PERIOD:
Early summer

**CATERPILLAR FOOD
PLANTS:**
Poplar (*Populus*)

This butterfly is found throughout northern
and central Europe, although it is less common
in the west and absent from N Scandinavia and
the British Isles. It prefers damp, open woodland up to around 1000 m, and spends its time
flying high up in the trees, coming down only
to feed from carrion and dung. The caterpillar
is brown at first, overwintering on a twig and
changing to green in spring when the leaves
begin to open.

caterpillar

J	F	M	A	M	J
J	A	S	O	N	D

Southern White Admiral
Limenitis reducta

ID FACT FILE

WINGSPAN:
4.6–5.4 cm

DESCRIPTION:
Very like White Admiral but only 1 row of black spots near edges of hindwings, not 2. Also forewings have 1 white spot closer to body

HIBERNATING STAGE:
Caterpillar

FLIGHT PERIOD:
Mid-spring to late summer

CATERPILLAR FOOD PLANTS:
Honeysuckle (*Lonicera*)

LOOKALIKES:
White Admiral (p.105)

This butterfly is fairly common throughout most of S Europe except S Spain. It can also be found in NW France, but there it is very rare. It prefers open woodland and forest edges up to around 1500 m. There are usually two or three broods each year, and the caterpillar is brown at first, changing to green later. Those of final brood spend the winter inside a folded leaf and change to green in the spring. The pupa looks like a small dried leaf

NYMPHALIDAE (BRUSH-FOOTED BUTTERFLIES)

J	F	M	A	M	J
J	A	S	O	N	D

Glanville Fritillary
Melitaea cinxia

ID FACT FILE

WINGSPAN:
3.2–4.3 cm

DESCRIPTION:
Light orange-brown with dark brown markings. Underside pale orange-brown with cream markings and black spots. Female larger and paler

HIBERNATING STAGE:
Caterpillar

FLIGHT PERIOD:
Late spring, also late summer in the south

CATERPILLAR FOOD PLANTS:
Plantain (*Plantago*)

A common butterfly throughout most of Europe, but it is absent from N Scandinavia and S Spain, while in the British Isles it is found only on the Isle of Wight. It prefers flowery meadows up to around 2000 m. The caterpillars live together in a communal silk tent when young – the overwintering brood hibernating within this tent – and separate when much larger. Larger caterpillars look very much like plantain flower heads.

caterpillar

NYMPHALIDAE (BRUSH-FOOTED BUTTERFLIES)

J	F	M	A	M	J
J	A	S	O	N	D

False Heath Fritillary
Melitaea diamina

ID FACT FILE

WINGSPAN:
3.4–4.2 cm

DESCRIPTION:
Dark brown with
orange-brown
spots, male hind-
wings mostly
brown. Underside
pale orange-
brown with
yellowish spots.
Female more
spotted, often
paler

**HIBERNATING
STAGE:**
Caterpillar

FLIGHT PERIOD:
Late spring to
early summer,
also mid-summer
in south

**CATERPILLAR FOOD
PLANTS:**
Plantain,
(*Plantago*),
speedwell
(*Veronica*) and
other low-growing
plants

This is a fairly common butterfly throughout
most of central and E Europe, also N Spain,
and with isolated colonies in S Scandinavia and
NW France. It prefers damp grassland areas
and woodland edges up to around 2000 m.
There may be one or two broods each year,
depending on locality, and the young caterpillars live together in a group within a silken
tent, separating as they grow larger or after
hibernation.

caterpillar

NYMPHALIDAE (BRUSH-FOOTED BUTTERFLIES)

J	F	M	A	M	J
J	A	S	O	N	D

Spotted Fritillary
Melitaea didyma

This very common butterfly is found right across central and S Europe, where it prefers sunny, flowery meadows, sometimes open woodland, up to around 2000 m. It is a very variable species and many different forms have been named. There may be one to three broods each year, depending on locality. Young caterpillars live together in a silk tent, the final brood of the year spending the winter within it, and they separate when larger.

ID FACT FILE

WINGSPAN:
3.6–4.4 cm

DESCRIPTION:
Light orange-brown with dark brown spots; underside similar to Glanville Fritillary (p.108). Female often paler

HIBERNATING STAGE:
Caterpillar

FLIGHT PERIOD:
Mid-spring to late summer

CATERPILLAR FOOD PLANTS:
Plantain (*Plantago*), speedwell (*Veronica*) and toadflax (*Linaria*)

LOOKALIKES:
Lesser Spotted Fritillary (p.112)

caterpillar

J	F	M	A	M	J
J	A	S	O	N	D

Knapweed Fritillary
Melitaea pheobe

ID FACT FILE

WINGSPAN:
4–4.8 cm

DESCRIPTION:
Light orange-brown with dark brown markings and yellowish spots. Underside similar but spots creamy yellow. Female larger

HIBERNATING STAGE:
Caterpillar

FLIGHT PERIOD:
Mid-spring to late summer, depending on locality

CATERPILLAR FOOD PLANTS:
Knapweed (*Centaurea*)

This butterfly is fairly common throughout central and S Europe, where it produces a number of different forms. It prefers flowery meadows up to around 2000 m, and may produce one to three broods each year, depending on locality. The caterpillars live together in a silk tent, separating when almost fully grown, and the final brood of the year will shelter within their tent through the winter. They pupate under a leaf of the food plant.

caterpillar

NYMPHALIDAE (BRUSH-FOOTED BUTTERFLIES)

J	F	M	A	M	J
J	A	S	O	N	D

Lesser Spotted Fritillary
Melitaea trivia

ID FACT FILE

WINGSPAN:
3.4–3.8 cm

DESCRIPTION:
Similar to Spotted Fritillary, but generally smaller and the underside markings not so dark

HIBERNATING STAGE:
Caterpillar

FLIGHT PERIOD:
Late spring and mid-summer

CATERPILLAR FOOD PLANTS:
Mullein (*Verbascum*)

LOOKALIKES:
Spotted Fritillary (p.110)

This butterfly is fairly common in E Europe, and there are scattered colonies from Italy to N Spain. It prefers flowery meadows and rough, open ground, usually in the hills and mountains up to around 1500 m. There are two broods each year, the caterpillars live together while young and make a silk tent in which to live, inside which the second brood will shelter through the winter. They will usually pupate under a leaf on the food plant.

caterpillar

J	F	M	A	M	J
J	A	S	O	N	D

Heath Fritillary
Mellicta athalia

ID FACT FILE

WINGSPAN:
3.4–4.6 cm

DESCRIPTION:
Light orange-brown, heavily marked with dark brown. Underside pale yellow with orange-brown markings and white spots. Female larger

HIBERNATING STAGE:
Caterpillar

FLIGHT PERIOD:
Mid-spring to late summer; 1–3 broods, depending on locality

CATERPILLAR FOOD PLANTS:
Cow-wheat (*Melampyrum*) and plantain (*Plantago*)

LOOKALIKES:
Meadow Fritillary (p.116), Nickerl's Fritillary (p.114) and Provençal Fritillary (p.115)

This common and very variable butterfly can be found throughout most of Europe, except for S Spain; and in the British Isles it is restricted to a few scattered colonies in S England. It prefers flowery meadows, open woodland and forest edges, up to around 2000 m. The caterpillars live in a group in a silk tent, spending the winter sheltering inside and separating when much larger. They pupate under a leaf of the food plant.

caterpillar

NYMPHALIDAE (BRUSH-FOOTED BUTTERFLIES)

J	F	M	A	M	J
J	A	S	O	N	D

Nickerl's Fritillary
Mellicta aurelia

ID FACT FILE

WINGSPAN:
2.8–3.2 cm

DESCRIPTION:
Very similar to
Heath Fritillary
but smaller and
not as heavily
marked

**HIBERNATING
STAGE:**
Caterpillar

FLIGHT PERIOD:
Early summer

**CATERPILLAR FOOD
PLANTS:**
Plantain (*Planta-
go*), cow-wheat
(*Melampyrum*)
and speedwell
(*Veronica*)

LOOKALIKES:
Heath Fritillary
(p.113) and
Meadow Fritillary
(p.116)

This butterfly is fairly common throughout
central and E Europe, where it prefers heaths,
meadows and moorland with an abundant
supply of flowers, up to around 1500 m. The
caterpillar is black with tiny white spots and
pale brown branched spines. When young the
caterpillars live in a group in a silk tent, spending the winter sheltering inside and separating
in the spring, when they can often be seen
basking in the sun.

caterpillar

J	F	M	A	M	J
J	A	S	O	N	D

Provençal Fritillary
Mellicta deione

ID FACT FILE

WINGSPAN:
4–4.5 cm

DESCRIPTION:
Very similar to
Heath Fritillary,
but can be recog-
nised by the
number of black
spots on the
underside of the
forewing

**HIBERNATING
STAGE:**
Caterpillar

FLIGHT PERIOD:
Late spring to
early summer
and late summer
to early autumn

**CATERPILLAR FOOD
PLANTS:**
Toadflax (*Linaria*)

LOOKALIKES:
Heath Fritillary
(p.113)

This butterfly is found only in south-western
Europe, from Spain and Portugal across to
N Italy. It usually prefers flowery fields and
meadows in hilly areas up to around 1700 m.
There are several different forms of this butterfly, and it can be easily confused with the
Heath Fritillary. The caterpillar is black with
tiny white spots, and covered with many light
brown branching spines. There are normally
two broods each year.

female

male

NYMPHALIDAE (BRUSH-FOOTED BUTTERFLIES)

J	F	M	A	M	J
J	A	S	O	N	D

Meadow Fritillary
Mellicta parthenoides

ID FACT FILE

WINGSPAN:
3.2–3.6 cm

DESCRIPTION:
Similar to both
Heath and
Nickerl's
Fritillaries but not
as heavily
marked as either
species. Female
paler

**HIBERNATING
STAGE:**
Caterpillar

FLIGHT PERIOD:
Late spring and
late summer,
early summer
only in
mountains

**CATERPILLAR FOOD
PLANTS:**
Plantain (*Plantago*) and scabious
(*Scabiosa*)

LOOKALIKES:
Heath Fritillary
(p.113) and
Nickerl's Fritillary
(p.114)

This butterfly is found only in W Europe, from
France, Switzerland and Italy across to Spain,
where it is probably commonest. It is mainly a
lowland species, though it can be found as high
as 2000 m, and it prefers damp, flowery meadows. There are usually two broods each year,
but in the mountains it produces only one. The
caterpillars are black with tiny white dots and
branched yellow spines, and live together in a
silk tent.

male

female

NYMPHALIDAE (BRUSH-FOOTED BUTTERFLIES)

J	F	M	A	M	J
J	A	S	O	N	D

Camberwell Beauty
Nymphalis antiopa

ID FACT FILE

WINGSPAN:
6–6.8 cm

DESCRIPTION:
Dark purple-
brown with a row
of blue spots
and yellow
edges.
Underside mostly
black with dark
cream edges.
Sexes alike

**HIBERNATING
STAGE:**
Adult

FLIGHT PERIOD:
Early to late
summer and
early to
mid-spring

**CATERPILLAR FOOD
PLANTS:**
Willow (*Salix*),
birch (*Betula*)
and elm (*Ulmus*)

This butterfly can be found throughout most of
Europe except the British Isles and S Spain,
but in the far north it is mainly just a migratory
summer visitor. It prefers open woodland and
rough, open ground, usually in the hills up to
around 2500 m, but it rarely visits flowers,
feeding instead from tree-sap and rotten fruit.
The caterpillars live in a group within a silk
tent, and only separate when fully grown and
ready to pupate.

caterpillar

NYMPHALIDAE (BRUSH-FOOTED BUTTERFLIES)

J	F	M	A	M	J
J	A	S	O	N	D

Large Tortoiseshell
Nymphalis polychloros

ID FACT FILE

WINGSPAN:
5–6.4 cm

DESCRIPTION:
Similar to Small
Tortoiseshell
but larger and
darker; blue
crescents on
hindwings only

**HIBERNATING
STAGE:**
Adult

FLIGHT PERIOD:
Early to late sum-
mer and early to
mid-spring

**CATERPILLAR FOOD
PLANTS:**
Elm (*Ulmus*), wil-
low (*Salix*) and
poplar (*Populus*)

LOOKALIKES:
Small Tortoise-
shell (p.84)

This butterfly is fairly common throughout
most of Europe, but is absent from N Scandinavia, and rare in the British Isles, being
restricted to parts of S England and Wales. It
prefers open woodland and forest edges up to
around 2000 m, and in spring can often be
seen feeding from sallow (*Salix*) catkins. The
caterpillars live together in a loose tent when
young, separating as they grow larger, and
pupating under a leaf of the food plant.

caterpillar

NYMPHALIDAE (BRUSH-FOOTED BUTTERFLIES)

J	F	M	A	M	J
J	A	S	O	N	D

Cardinal
Pandoriana pandora

ID FACT FILE

WINGSPAN:
6.4–8 cm

DESCRIPTION:
Very similar to
Silver-washed
Fritillary but
underside
forewings have
pinkish-red
patch.

**HIBERNATING
STAGE:**
Caterpillar

FLIGHT PERIOD:
Early summer

**CATERPILLAR FOOD
PLANTS:**
Violet (*Viola*)

LOOKALIKES:
Silver-washed
Fritillary (p.92)

This is the largest of the European Fritillaries, and is fairly common throughout the southern half of the continent. It prefers flowery meadows and woodland edges up to around 2000 m, and is very fond of thistle (*Carduus*) flowers. The caterpillar is brown, with a wide black band streaked with grey down the back, and rows of branched brown spines. It feeds at night and when fully grown pupates under a leaf of the food plant.

male

▲ female underside

NYMPHALIDAE (BRUSH-FOOTED BUTTERFLIES)

J	F	M	A	M	J
J	A	S	O	N	D

Comma
Polygonia c-album

ID FACT FILE

WINGSPAN:
4.4–4.8 cm

DESCRIPTION:
Bright orange-
brown with dark
brown spots and
edges. Under-
side dark brown
with green
markings and
white 'comma'
on hindwing.
Sexes alike

**HIBERNATING
STAGE:**
Adult

FLIGHT PERIOD:
Mid-summer to
early autumn and
early to late
spring

**CATERPILLAR FOOD
PLANTS:**
Nettle (*Urtica*),
hop (*Humulus*)
and elm (*Ulmus*)

This is a common butterfly found throughout
most of Europe except for the far north. In the
British Isles it is found only in S England and
Wales. It prefers open woodland, hedgerows,
parks and gardens, up to around 2000 m.
There are two broods each year, and adults of
the first generation are generally paler than
those of the second. The caterpillar is brown
with black markings and a large white patch on
the back.

left 2nd brood
right 1st brood

J	F	M	A	M	J
J	A	S	O	N	D

Bog Fritillary
Proclossiana eunomia

ID FACT FILE

WINGSPAN:
3.2–4.6 cm

DESCRIPTION:
Light orange-brown with dark brown markings. Underside sandy with orange-brown and pale yellow or silvery spots. Sexes alike

HIBERNATING STAGE:
Caterpillar

FLIGHT PERIOD:
Early summer

CATERPILLAR FOOD PLANTS:
Bistort (*Polygonum*) and cranberry (*Vaccinium*)

This butterfly is fairly common in NE Europe, but in France, Germany, Austria and Bulgaria it exists only in widely scattered and very local colonies. It prefers peat-bogs and fenlands up to around 1500 m. There is only one brood each year, and in the coldest areas the life-cycle may take two years, with the caterpillars living through two winters. During the warmest days the caterpillars may often be seen basking in the sun.

caterpillar

J	F	M	A	M	J
J	A	S	O	N	D

Red Admiral
Vanessa atalanta

ID FACT FILE

WINGSPAN:
5.6–6.2 cm

DESCRIPTION:
Black with red bands and white spots. Underside mostly dark brown mottled black and blue. Sexes alike

HIBERNATING STAGE:
Adult, rarely surviving winter in the north

FLIGHT PERIOD:
Late spring to early autumn and early to mid-spring

CATERPILLAR FOOD PLANTS:
Nettle (*Urtica*)

This common butterfly is resident only in S Europe, but every year it migrates northwards, reaching every part of the continent. It can be found wherever there are flowers, and is a common sight in gardens. In the autumn it is strongly attracted to rotten fruit. The caterpillar lives inside a folded leaf all through its development, and when fully grown often wanders some distance from the food plant before pupating.

caterpillar

Nettle-Tree Butterfly
Libythea celtis

ID FACT FILE

SUB-FAMILY:
Libytheinae
(Snout
butterflies)

WINGSPAN:
3.4–4.4 cm

DESCRIPTION:
Dark brown with
light orange-
brown patches
and 1 whIte spot
on each
forewing. Under-
side looks like
an old brown
leaf. Sexes alike

**HIBERNATING
STAGE:**
Adult

FLIGHT PERIOD:
Early to late
summer and
early to late
spring

**CATERPILLAR FOOD
PLANTS:**
Nettle tree
(*Celtis*)

This easily recognised butterfly is fairly
common in S Europe, where it can be found in
open woodland and scrubland, wherever the
food plant grows. It is a lowland species, rarely
seen higher than 1000 m except in late
summer, when it tends to migrate short distances. The butterfly is on the wing for most of
the summer, but does not mate or lay eggs
until the following spring. The caterpillars
usually live in small groups.

caterpillars

NYMPHALIDAE (BRUSH-FOOTED BUTTERFLIES)

J	F	M	A	M	J
J	A	S	O	N	D

Ringlet
Aphantopus hyperantus

ID FACT FILE

SUB-FAMILY:
Satyrinae (Satyrs and wood nymphs)

WINGSPAN:
4–4.8 cm

DESCRIPTION:
Very dark brown with 1 or 2 black eye-like markings on each wing. Underside dark brown with several yellow-ringed black eye-spots. Sexes alike

HIBERNATING STAGE:
Caterpillar

FLIGHT PERIOD:
Early summer

CATERPILLAR FOOD PLANTS:
Various grasses

This butterfly is common throughout most of Europe, but is absent from N Scandinavia and N Scotland, also most of Spain and Italy. It prefers open woodland, hedgerows and damp meadows up to around 1500 m, and is very fond of bramble (*Rubus*) flowers. The female scatters her eggs while flying over grassy areas, and the resulting caterpillars feed mainly at night. When fully grown they pupate on the ground in a flimsy cocoon.

caterpillar

J	F	M	A	M	J
J	A	S	O	N	D

False Grayling
Arethusana arethusa

ID FACT FILE

SUB-FAMILY:
Satyrinae (Satyrs and wood nymphs)

WINGSPAN:
4.4–4.8 cm

DESCRIPTION:
Mid-brown with a band of pale orange-brown spots and a single black spot on each wing. Male has only one spot on forewings. Underside of both sexes mainly pale brown with a white band

HIBERNATING STAGE:
Caterpillar

FLIGHT PERIOD:
Mid-summer

CATERPILLAR FOOD PLANTS:
Various grasses, especially *Festuca*

This butterfly is found in central and S Europe, where it is locally common on dry heaths and other grassy places, mainly on chalk soils, up to around 1800 m. It often settles on bare ground, where, with wings closed, it is very difficult to spot. The caterpillar is pale brown or grey with a darker line down the back and sides. In spring when fully grown it pupates on the ground amongst grass roots and leaf-litter.

male underside

left male
right female

NYMPHALIDAE (BRUSH-FOOTED BUTTERFLIES)

Great Banded Grayling
Brintesia circe

ID FACT FILE

SUB-FAMILY:
Satyrinae (Satyrs and wood nymphs)

WINGSPAN:
6.6–7.2 cm

DESCRIPTION:
Very dark brown with a wide band of pure white spots. Underside similar. Sexes alike

HIBERNATING STAGE:
Caterpillar

FLIGHT PERIOD:
Early summer

CATERPILLAR FOOD PLANTS:
Various grasses

This large butterfly is found throughout central and S Europe, and towards the east it is also found further north. It prefers open woodland up to around 1800 m, and is very fond of basking in the sun on trunks, rocks and bare earth, where it is well camouflaged and can be very difficult to see. The caterpillar, too, is well camouflaged, feeding mainly at night and pupating, when fully grown, on the food plant.

caterpillar

NYMPHALIDAE (BRUSH-FOOTED BUTTERFLIES)

J	F	M	A	M	J
J	A	S	O	N	D

Hermit
Charaza briseis

ID FACT FILE

SUB-FAMILY:
Satyrinae (Satyrs and wood nymphs)

WINGSPAN:
4.2–6 cm

DESCRIPTION:
Dark brown with a band of white spots and 2 black eye-spots on the forewings. Underside similar but much paler. Female darker and larger

HIBERNATING STAGE:
Caterpillar

FLIGHT PERIOD:
Early to mid-summer

CATERPILLAR FOOD PLANTS:
Various grasses

A fairly common butterfly found right across central and S Europe, with the exception of Portugal and W Spain. It prefers dry grassland up to 2000 m, where it can settle on patches of bare earth to bask in the sun. It is also fond of feeding from scabious (*Scabiosa*) flowers. The caterpillar has a pale brown head and dark bluish-green striped body, and feeds mainly at night. It pupates amongst grass roots.

male underside

left male
right female

NYMPHALIDAE (BRUSH-FOOTED BUTTERFLIES)

J	F	M	A	M	J
J	A	S	O	N	D

Pearly Heath
Coenonympha arcania

ID FACT FILE

SUB-FAMILY:
Satyrinae (Satyrs and wood nymphs)

WINGSPAN:
3.2–4 cm

DESCRIPTION:
Forewings orange-brown, hindwings darker, all edged smoky brown. Underside pale brown with white band and several yellow-ringed eye-spots. Sexes alike

HIBERNATING STAGE:
Caterpillar

FLIGHT PERIOD:
Early summer

CATERPILLAR FOOD PLANTS:
Various grasses

This fairly common butterfly is found throughout most of central and S Europe, also S Scandinavia, but is absent from S Spain. It is a grassland species, although it can be seen in open woodland, and is probably commonest in the hills and mountains up to around 2000 m. There is usually only one brood each year, rarely a second, partial brood in the south. The green or brown pupa is attached to a grass stem.

caterpillar

NYMPHALIDAE (BRUSH-FOOTED BUTTERFLIES)

J	F	M	A	M	J
J	A	S	O	N	D

Chestnut Heath
Coenonympha glycerion

ID FACT FILE

SUB-FAMILY:
Satyrinae (Satyrs and wood nymphs)

WINGSPAN:
3.2–3.6 cm

DESCRIPTION:
Plain mid-brown, female paler with orange-brown patch on forewings. Underside pale brown with white band and several eye-spots on hindwings

HIBERNATING STAGE:
Caterpillar

FLIGHT PERIOD:
Early summer

CATERPILLAR FOOD PLANTS:
Various grasses

LOOKALIKES:
Small Heath (p.130) and Large Heath (p.131)

This butterfly is found mainly in E and NE Europe with a few scattered colonies in N Spain and SW France, but it is a rather local species. It prefers open grassland areas, generally in the hills and mountains up to around 2000 m. The caterpillar is green with a darker line down the back and a cream stripe along each side, and it feeds mainly at night. The green pupa is attached to a grass stem.

left male
right female

NYMPHALIDAE (BRUSH-FOOTED BUTTERFLIES)

| J | F | M | A | M | J |
| J | A | S | O | N | D |

Small Heath
Coenonympha pamphilus

ID FACT FILE

Sub-family:
Satyrinae (Satyrs and wood nymphs)

Wingspan:
2.6–3.2 cm

Description:
Light orange-brown with brown edges and a black spot on each forewing. Underside pale brownish-grey with a short white band and an eye-spot on each forewing. Female larger

Hibernating stage:
Caterpillar

Flight period:
Mid-spring to early autumn, depending on locality

Caterpillar food plants:
Various grasses

Lookalikes:
Large Heath (p.131) and Chestnut Heath (p.129)

This very common butterfly is found throughout Europe except the far north, and prefers meadows, heaths and any other kind of rough grassy areas, up to around 2000 m. There may be up to three broods each year, depending on locality, but some caterpillars from each of the first broods will hibernate along with all those of the last brood. The caterpillar usually feeds during the day, and later attaches itself to a grass stem to pupate.

caterpillar

NYMPHALIDAE (BRUSH-FOOTED BUTTERFLIES)

J	F	M	A	M	J
J	A	S	O	N	D

Large Heath
Coenonympha tullia

ID FACT FILE

SUB-FAMILY:
Satyrinae (Satyrs and wood nymphs)

WINGSPAN:
3–4 cm

DESCRIPTION:
Male, smoky orange-brown; female paler. Underside of both sexes pale brown with a variable white band and several eyespots, including 2 on each forewing

HIBERNATING STAGE:
Caterpillar

FLIGHT PERIOD:
Early summer

CATERPILLAR FOOD PLANTS:
Various grasses

LOOKALIKES:
Chestnut Heath (p.129) and Small Heath (p.130)

This very variable butterfly is found throughout most of E and NE Europe, except for the far north of Scandinavia. In the British Isles it can be seen everywhere except S England. It prefers bogs, moorland and damp grassland up to around 2500 m. The caterpillar, which is green with a darker line along the back and two pale stripes down each side, feeds mainly at night. The pupa is green with black streaks and is attached to a grass stem.

left male
right female

NYMPHALIDAE (BRUSH-FOOTED BUTTERFLIES)

| J | F | M | A | M | J |
| J | A | S | O | N | D |

Scotch Argus
Erebia aethiops

ID FACT FILE

SUB-FAMILY:
Satyrinae (Satyrs and wood nymphs)

WINGSPAN:
4.4–5.2 cm

DESCRIPTION:
Very dark brown with an orange-brown band on each wing marked with several eye-spots. Underside similar but hindwing band greyish. Female paler

HIBERNATING STAGE:
Caterpillar

FLIGHT PERIOD:
Late summer

CATERPILLAR FOOD PLANTS:
Various grasses

This butterfly is found mainly in E Europe, with some scattered colonies in N Italy, France, N England and Scotland. It prefers open grassland, often around the edges of pine forests and usually in the hills and mountains up to around 2000 m, flying only when the sun is shining. The caterpillar, which is pale brown with a darker line along the back and sides, feeds at dawn and dusk, later pupating in a flimsy cocoon amongst leaf-litter.

male of European race

Scottish race
left female
right male

NYMPHALIDAE (BRUSH-FOOTED BUTTERFLIES)

J	F	M	A	M	J
J	A	S	O	N	D

Arran Brown
Erebia ligea

ID FACT FILE

SUB-FAMILY:
Satyrinae (Satyrs and wood nymphs)

WINGSPAN:
4.2–5.4 cm

DESCRIPTION:
Very dark brown with an orange-brown band marked with several eye-spots. Underside similar but band on hind-wings white. Female paler

HIBERNATING STAGE:
Caterpillar

FLIGHT PERIOD:
Early summer

CATERPILLAR FOOD PLANTS:
Various grasses

A fairly common butterfly in E Europe and also Scandinavia and Finland, but in France and Italy it is restricted to scattered local colonies. Very much a hillside and mountain species, it prefers meadows, heaths and open woodland between 500m and 1500 m, living in the lowlands only in the far north. The caterpillar is pale brown with a darker line down the back, and in colder areas may hibernate twice before completing its growth.

male

female

NYMPHALIDAE (BRUSH-FOOTED BUTTERFLIES)

Woodland Ringlet
Erebia medusa

J	F	M	A	M	J
J	A	S	O	N	D

ID FACT FILE

SUB-FAMILY:
Satyrinae (Satyrs and wood nymphs)

WINGSPAN:
3.8–5 cm

DESCRIPTION:
Dark brown with several eye-spots on each wing outlined in orange-brown. Underside similar. Female paler

HIBERNATING STAGE:
Caterpillar

FLIGHT PERIOD:
Early summer

CATERPILLAR FOOD PLANTS:
Various grasses

This butterfly is fairly common in central and SE Europe, where it prefers damp meadows and moorland, often around woodland edges. In the north it is usually found in the lowlands, but everywhere else it is a hillside and mountain species, found up to around 2000 m. The caterpillar may be either green or brown, and feeds mainly at night, often hibernating through two winters in colder areas before pupating on the ground amongst leaf-litter.

caterpillar

J	F	M	A	M	J
J	A	S	O	N	D

Dewy Ringlet
Erebia pandrose

ID FACT FILE

SUB-FAMILY:
Satyrinae (Satyrs and wood nymphs)

WINGSPAN:
4–5 cm

DESCRIPTION:
Dark brown with an orange-brown patch on the forewings and several small black eye-spots. Underside silvery-grey with thin brown wavy lines. Female paler

HIBERNATING STAGE:
Caterpillar

FLIGHT PERIOD:
Early summer

CATERPILLAR FOOD PLANTS:
Various grasses

This butterfly is found mainly in N Scandinavia with scattered local colonies in the mountain districts of S Europe, from the Pyrenees eastwards. It prefers rough, open ground and mountain pastures up to 3000 m, but is only found in the lowlands in the north. As with many other *Erebia* butterflies, it flies only when the sun is shining. When fully grown the caterpillar pupates on the ground amongst grass roots and leaf-litter.

caterpillar

J	F	M	A	M	J
J	A	S	O	N	D

Rock Grayling
Hipparchia alcyone

ID FACT FILE

SUB-FAMILY:
Satyrinae (Satyrs and wood nymphs)

WINGSPAN:
5.4–6.8 cm

DESCRIPTION:
Dark grey-brown with a pale brown band (white in the female), and an eye-spot on each forewing. Underside dark brown near the body, pale brown and white on the outer half

HIBERNATING STAGE:
Caterpillar

FLIGHT PERIOD:
Early summer

CATERPILLAR FOOD PLANTS:
Various grasses

LOOKALIKES:
Woodland Grayling (p.137)

A fairly common butterfly in southern and central Europe and also S Scandinavia; it prefers rough, stony ground. In the north it lives in the lowlands, but in the south it is restricted to scattered colonies in the mountains, up to 2000 m. The caterpillar, which feeds at night, is pale greyish-brown with a darker stripe down the back and two thin lines along each side. It pupates on the ground in a loose cocoon.

left female
right male

NYMPHALIDAE (BRUSH-FOOTED BUTTERFLIES)

J	F	M	A	M	J
J	A	S	O	N	D

Woodland Grayling
Hipparchia fagi

ID FACT FILE

SUB-FAMILY:
Satyrinae (Satyrs and wood nymphs)

WINGSPAN:
6.6–7.6 cm

DESCRIPTION:
Very similar to Rock Grayling but larger

HIBERNATING STAGE:
Caterpillar

FLIGHT PERIOD:
Mid-summer

CATERPILLAR FOOD PLANTS:
Various grasses

LOOKALIKES:
Rock Grayling (p.136)

This butterfly is common locally throughout central and S Europe, but is absent from Portugal and S Spain. It prefers open woodland up to around 1000 m, and often sits on a tree trunk to bask in the sun, where it can be very hard to spot. The caterpillar is pale brown with a dark stripe along the back and a thin line down the sides. It feeds at night, and when fully grown, pupates on the ground amongst leaf-litter.

mating pair

left male
right female

J	F	M	A	M	J
J	A	S	O	N	D

Grayling
Hipparchia semele

ID FACT FILE

SUB-FAMILY:
Satyrinae (Satyrs and wood nymphs)

WINGSPAN:
4.2–6 cm

DESCRIPTION:
Mid-brown with a paler band and 2 eye-spots on the forewings, 1 on the hindwings. Underside similar but with a whitish band on the hindwings. Female darker, bands on upper-side yellow

HIBERNATING STAGE:
Caterpillar

FLIGHT PERIOD:
Mid-summer

CATERPILLAR FOOD PLANTS:
Various grasses

This butterfly is found throughout Europe except S Italy and N Scandinavia. In the British Isles it is mainly restricted to coastal areas. It prefers heathland, sand hills and open woodland, up to around 2000 m, and is very hard to see when it settles on a patch of bare earth. The caterpillar is pale brown with darker stripes along the back and sides. It feeds mainly at night, and pupates in a flimsy cocoon on the ground.

male

NYMPHALIDAE (BRUSH-FOOTED BUTTERFLIES)

Dusky Meadow Brown
Hyponephele lycaon

ID FACT FILE

SUB-FAMILY:
Satyrinae (Satyrs and wood nymphs)

WINGSPAN:
4–4.8 cm

DESCRIPTION:
Similar to Meadow Brown, but slightly smaller and generally more orange on upperside of both sexes. Female has 2 eye-spots on forewings

HIBERNATING STAGE:
Caterpillar

FLIGHT PERIOD:
Mid-summer

CATERPILLAR FOOD PLANTS:
Various grasses

LOOKALIKES:
Meadow Brown (p.144)

This butterfly is found in S and E Europe, reaching as far north in the east as Finland, but it is absent from the south-western corner of Spain and Portugal. It prefers dry, rocky grassland, usually in the lowlands, but can be seen up to around 2000 m. The caterpillar is green with pale yellow stripes along the back and sides. The pupa may be either green or brown and is attached to a grass stem. Females usually hatch later than males.

left male
right female

J	F	M	A	M	J
J	A	S	O	N	D

Large Wall Brown
Lasiommata maera

This is a fairly common butterfly throughout most of Europe, but it is not found in N Scandinavia or the British Isles. It prefers open woodland, forest edges and dry grassland, usually in the hills, up to around 2000 m, and likes to bask in the sun on a stone or tree trunk. The caterpillar is green with several paler lines along the back and sides. The pupa is green or brown and attached to a grass stem close to the ground.

ID FACT FILE

SUB-FAMILY:
Satyrinae (Satyrs and wood nymphs)

WINGSPAN:
5–5.6 cm

DESCRIPTION:
Dark brown with orange-ringed eye-spots. Female orange markings brighter and more extensive. Underside of both sexes greyish-brown with a row of small eye-spots on hindwings; single large spot on forewings

HIBERNATING STAGE:
Caterpillar

FLIGHT PERIOD:
Late spring and late summer in the south; early summer in the north

CATERPILLAR FOOD PLANTS:
Various grasses

LOOKALIKES:
Northern Wall Brown (p.142)

female

male

NYMPHALIDAE (BRUSH-FOOTED BUTTERFLIES)

J	F	M	A	M	J
J	A	S	O	N	D

Wall Brown
Lasiommata megera

ID FACT FILE

Sub-family:
Satyrinae (Satyrs and wood nymphs)

Wingspan:
3.6–5 cm

Description:
Dark brown with large orange-brown spots, one eye-spot on the forewings, and several on the hindwings. Underside pale brown with smaller eye-spots. Female paler

Hibernating stage:
Caterpillar

Flight period:
Early spring to late summer; 2 or 3 broods

Caterpillar food plants:
Various grasses

This is a common butterfly in most of Europe, but it is absent from Finland and N Scandinavia. It prefers heathland and other grasslands, open woodland and gardens, up to around 2000 m, and likes to bask in the sun on stones or open ground. The caterpillar is green with whitish lines along the back and sides, and feeds mainly at night. The pupa is usually green but may be marked with black, and is attached to a grass stem.

male

female

NYMPHALIDAE (BRUSH-FOOTED BUTTERFLIES)

J	F	M	A	M	J
J	A	S	O	N	D

Northern Wall Brown
Lasiommata petropolitana

ID FACT FILE

SUB-FAMILY:
Satyrinae (Satyrs and wood nymphs)

WINGSPAN:
3.8–4.2 cm

DESCRIPTION:
Similar to Large Wall Brown but smaller and with more orange, especially in the female

HIBERNATING STAGE:
Pupa in the north; caterpillar in the south

FLIGHT PERIOD:
Late spring to early summer

CATERPILLAR FOOD PLANTS:
Various grasses

LOOKALIKES:
Large Wall Brown (p.140)

This butterfly is mainly found in the countries around the Baltic Sea, particularly Scandinavia and Finland; in this area it is a lowland species, but it is also found in widely scattered colonies in the mountains of S Europe up to an altitude of around 2000 m. It prefers clearings in pine woodland where it is usually seen basking in the sun. The caterpillar is green with paler stripes, while the pupa is plain green and is attached to a grass stem.

female

left male
right female

NYMPHALIDAE (BRUSH-FOOTED BUTTERFLIES)

J	F	M	A	M	J
J	A	S	O	N	D

Woodland Brown
Lopinga achine

ID FACT FILE

SUB-FAMILY:
Satyrinae (Satyrs and wood nymphs)

WINGSPAN:
5–5.4 cm

DESCRIPTION:
Dark brown; each wing has several eye-spots ringed with creamy yellow. Underside similar but with more markings in yellow and also white. Sexes alike

HIBERNATING STAGE:
Caterpillar

FLIGHT PERIOD:
Early summer

CATERPILLAR FOOD PLANTS:
Various grasses

This butterfly is locally common in widely scattered colonies, mainly across central Europe and normally in the lowlands. It is a shade-loving woodland species, and is rarely seen flying in sunlight. Usually the females tend to emerge slightly later than the males. The green caterpillars can be found – with difficulty – feeding during the day, while the pupa, which is green with white markings, is attached to a grass stem.

caterpillar

NYMPHALIDAE (BRUSH-FOOTED BUTTERFLIES)

J	F	M	A	M	J
J	A	S	O	N	D

Meadow Brown
Maniola jurtina

ID FACT FILE

SUB-FAMILY:
Satyrinae (Satyrs and wood nymphs)

WINGSPAN:
4.2–5.4 cm

DESCRIPTION:
Dark brown with 1 eye-spot on each forewing, female marked with orange-brown. Underside light brown with a paler band

HIBERNATING STAGE:
Caterpillar

FLIGHT PERIOD:
Late spring to late summer

CATERPILLAR FOOD PLANTS:
Various grasses

LOOKALIKES:
Dusky Meadow Brown (p.139)

This variable butterfly is very common throughout Europe, but is absent from N Scandinavia and Finland. It is found in all grassy places, including open woodland and forest edges, up to around 2000 m, and is often seen flying even on dull days. The caterpillar feeds mainly at night and is green with a darker line down the back and a thin, pale line along the sides. The green pupa is attached to a grass stem.

left male
right female

J	F	M	A	M	J
J	A	S	O	N	D

Marbled White
Melanargia galathea

ID FACT FILE

SUB-FAMILY:
Satyrinae (Satyrs and wood nymphs)

WINGSPAN:
4.6–5.6 cm

DESCRIPTION:
Black with large white, sometimes yellowish, spots. Underside similar but paler with several small eye-spots. Sexes alike

HIBERNATING STAGE:
Caterpillar

FLIGHT PERIOD:
Early summer

CATERPILLAR FOOD PLANTS:
Various grasses

This is a fairly common butterfly throughout central and S Europe, and is also found in the British Isles, mainly in S England and Wales. It can be found in most flowery grasslands up to around 2000 m. The female drops her eggs in flight, and the newly hatched caterpillars go straight into hibernation without feeding. They may be pale brown or green in colour, and in spring they feed mainly during the night, later pupating on the ground.

caterpillar

J	F	M	A	M	J
J	A	S	O	N	D

Dryad
Minois dryas

ID FACT FILE

Sub-family:
Satyrinae (Satyrs and wood nymphs)

Wingspan:
5.4–5.8 cm

Description:
Dark brown; each forewing has 2 large blue-centred eye-spots ringed with yellow. Under-side similar with a pale band on the hindwings. Female larger and paler

Hibernating stage:
Caterpillar

Flight period:
Mid-summer

Caterpillar food plants:
Various grasses

This butterfly is locally fairly common across most of central Europe and also some parts of the south. It mainly prefers dry, open woodland and grassland up to around 1500 m, although it can also be found in some fenland areas. The caterpillar is yellowish-grey with darker lines along the back and sides and a brown head. It usually feeds at night, and when fully grown it pupates on the ground amongst leaf-litter.

female underside

male

J	F	M	A	M	J
J	A	S	O	N	D

Tree Grayling
Neohipparchia statilinus

ID FACT FILE

SUB-FAMILY:
Satyrinae (Satyrs and wood nymphs)

WINGSPAN:
4.4–5.6 cm

DESCRIPTION:
Dark brown with 2 black eye-spots on each forewing. Under-side lighter with a whitish band. Female paler

HIBERNATING STAGE:
Caterpillar

FLIGHT PERIOD:
Mid- to late summer

CATERPILLAR FOOD PLANTS:
Various grasses

This butterfly can be found throughout central and S Europe, but it is rather local in many places. It prefers heaths and other shrubby grasslands, also open woodland, up to around 1500 m, often settling on a tree trunk where it is very hard to see. The caterpillar is pale brown striped with dark green and dark brown, and feeds mainly at night. When fully grown in late spring it pupates on the ground amongst leaf-litter.

female underside

male

J	F	M	A	M	J
J	A	S	O	N	D

Speckled Wood
Pararge aegeria

ID FACT FILE

SUB-FAMILY:
Satyrinae (Satyrs and wood nymphs)

WINGSPAN:
3.8–4.4 cm

DESCRIPTION:
Dark brown with cream spots in the north, orange-brown spots in the south, and several eye-spots. Underside marbled light and dark brown. Sexes alike

HIBERNATING STAGE:
Both caterpillar and pupa

FLIGHT PERIOD:
Early spring to early autumn, depending on locality

CATERPILLAR FOOD PLANTS:
Various grasses

A common butterfly throughout most of Europe, except the far north, with two distinct colour forms. It prefers shady wood-land up to around 1200 m. Males are very territorial, and will fiercely defend a patch of sunlight. There may be two or three broods each year, depending on locality. The caterpillar is green with a darker stripe down the back and paler lines along the sides. The green pupa is attached to a grass stem.

northern race

left southern race

NYMPHALIDAE (BRUSH-FOOTED BUTTERFLIES)

J	F	M	A	M	J
J	A	S	O	N	D

ID FACT FILE

SUB-FAMILY:
Satyrinae (Satyrs and wood nymphs)

WINGSPAN:
3–3.2 cm

DESCRIPTION:
Very similar to Gatekeeper but slightly smaller and has no eye-spots on hind-wing undersides

HIBERNATING STAGE:
Caterpillar

FLIGHT PERIOD:
Late spring to mid-summer; 2 broods

CATERPILLAR FOOD PLANTS:
Various grasses

LOOKALIKES:
Gatekeeper (p.150)

Southern Gatekeeper
Pyronia cecilia

This fairly common butterfly is found only in the southern parts of Europe, from Spain across to Greece and Turkey. It prefers dry, shrubby grasslands mainly in lowland areas, but can be seen up to around 1500 m, and is very fond of marjoram (*Origanum*) flowers. The caterpillar is pale brown with darker stripes along the back and sides, and usually feeds at night. The pupa is pale brown with black spots and is attached to a grass stem.

left male
right female

NYMPHALIDAE (BRUSH-FOOTED BUTTERFLIES)

J	F	M	A	M	J
J	A	S	O	N	D

Gatekeeper
Pyronia tithonus

ID FACT FILE

SUB--FAMILY:
Satyrinae (Satyrs and wood nymphs)

WINGSPAN:
3.4–3.8 cm

DESCRIPTION:
Mid-brown with large orange-brown patches and 1 eye-spot on each forewing. Underside lighter, hindwing with several small eye-spots and marbled with pale brown. Female paler

HIBERNATING STAGE:
Caterpillar

FLIGHT PERIOD:
Mid-summer

CATERPILLAR FOOD PLANTS:
Various grasses

LOOKALIKES:
Southern Gatekeeper (p.149)

Also known as the Hedge Brown, this very common butterfly is found throughout central and S Europe, also S England, Ireland and Wales. It prefers open woodland, hedgerows and grassland below 1000 m, and is very fond of bramble (*Rubus*) flowers. The caterpillar is pale brown with a darker stripe down the back and a pale line along the sides, and feeds mainly at night. The pale brown pupa is attached to a grass stem.

male

female

THYATIRIDAE (LUTESTRING MOTHS)

Buff Arches
Habrosyne pyritoides

ID FACT FILE

WINGSPAN:
3.5–4 cm

DESCRIPTION:
Forewings pale
greyish-brown
marked with an
angular pattern
in white and pale
brown; hindwings
pale grey. Sexes
alike

**HIBERNATING
STAGE:**
Pupa

FLIGHT PERIOD:
Early summer

**CATERPILLAR FOOD
PLANTS:**
Bramble and
raspberry
(*Rubus*)

This moth is locally common in most of central
and N Europe, except Scotland and N Scandinavia; it is also found in S France and N Italy.
It prefers woodland areas, parks and gardens,
particularly places with plenty of low-growing
shrubby plants. There is usually one brood
each year but there may sometimes be a second partial brood in the south. When fully
grown the caterpillar pupates underground in a
flimsy cocoon.

caterpillar

THYATIRIDAE (LUTESTRING MOTHS)

J	F	M	A	M	J
J	A	S	O	N	D

Peach Blossom
Thyatira batis

ID FACT FILE

WINGSPAN:
3.2–3.8 cm

DESCRIPTION:
Forewings dark brown with white spots which have pink centres; hindwings pale grey. Sexes alike

HIBERNATING STAGE:
Pupa

FLIGHT PERIOD:
Early summer in the north, late spring and late summer in the south

CATERPILLAR FOOD PLANTS:
Bramble and raspberry (*Rubus*)

This beautiful moth is common throughout most of central and N Europe, although in Scotland and other northern areas it is more local. It prefers woodlands, parks and gardens with plenty of low, bushy undergrowth where the moth easily hides away. There is only one brood each year in the north, but usually two further south. The caterpillar feeds at night, sometimes becoming a pest in gardens. When fully grown it pupates in a cocoon amongst leaf-litter.

caterpillar

DREPANIDAE (HOOK-TIP MOTHS)

J	F	M	A	M	J
J	A	S	O	N	D

Chinese Character
Cilix glaucata

ID FACT FILE

WINGSPAN:
1.8–2.2 cm

DESCRIPTION:
Mainly white, with a broad greyish-brown mark in the middle of the forewings and a row of small dots along the outer edge. The hindwings have a pale grey border. Sexes alike

HIBERNATING STAGE:
Pupa

FLIGHT PERIOD:
Mid-spring and mid-summer

CATERPILLAR FOOD PLANTS:
Hawthorn (*Crataegus*), sloe (*Prunus*) and related fruit trees

This moth is common throughout most of central and S Europe, and is also found in the British Isles. It prefers woodland edges and hedgerows. The 'hook' tips that most others in this family have are missing in this species, but the black and white pattern means that it looks very much like a bird-dropping when resting. There are two broods each year. When fully grown the caterpillar pupates in a cocoon amongst the leaves of the food plant or under the bark.

caterpillar

DREPANIDAE (HOOK-TIP MOTHS)

| J | F | M | A | M | J |
| J | A | S | O | N | D |

Pebble Hook-tip
Drepana falcataria

ID FACT FILE

WINGSPAN:
2.7–3.5 cm

DESCRIPTION:
Pale brown with
slightly darker
wavy lines
across all wings.
Slate-grey spot in
centre of each
forewing, with a
heavy, dark
brown line just
below this lead-
ing to the tip.
Sexes alike

**HIBERNATING
STAGE:**
Pupa

FLIGHT PERIOD:
Mid-spring and
mid-summer

**CATERPILLAR FOOD
PLANTS:**
Birch (*Betula*)
and alder (*Alnus*)

This is a common moth throughout most of
Europe, found mainly in deciduous woodland
areas and shrubby heathland, and also, increasingly, in parks, where birch trees are so often
planted for their decorative effect. The moth is
difficult to spot because it looks very much like
a dried leaf when at rest. There are two broods
each year. The caterpillar is usually found on
young plants and when fully grown makes a
cocoon in between two leaves.

caterpillar

J	F	M	A	M	J
J	A	S	O	N	D

Scalloped Hook-tip
Falcaria lacertinaria

ID FACT FILE

WINGSPAN:
2.7–3.5 cm

DESCRIPTION:
Forewings strongly scalloped, pale brown, darkening towards the tips, with 2 darker lines across the middle; hindwings creamy white. Female paler

HIBERNATING STAGE:
Caterpillar

FLIGHT PERIOD:
Late spring and late summer

CATERPILLAR FOOD PLANTS:
Birch (*Betula*) and alder (*Alnus*)

This moth is common throughout most of Europe, but in the south it is found mainly in the mountains. It prefers open woodland, but it can also be seen in heathland and commons. There are two broods each year, and the second generation usually produces larger adults. The odd-looking humped caterpillar is pale brown with darker brown markings, and when fully grown makes a loose cocoon amongst the leaves of its food plant.

caterpillar

GEOMETRIDAE (GEOMETER MOTHS)

Magpie
Abraxas grossulariata

| J | F | M | A | M | J |
| J | A | S | O | N | D |

ID FACT FILE

WINGSPAN:
3.5–4 cm

DESCRIPTION:
Yellow body with yellow line across each forewing, otherwise wings clear white with variable black spots. Female larger

HIBERNATING STAGE:
Caterpillar

FLIGHT PERIOD:
Late spring to early summer

CATERPILLAR FOOD PLANTS:
Sloe (*Prunus*), hawthorn (*Crataegus*), gooseberry (*Ribes*) and other currant bushes

The Magpie is a common moth throughout Europe, sometimes very common indeed, and is quite an eye-catching sight, so brightly is it coloured. This bold pattern means, of course, that the moth is poisonous (i.e. tastes nasty), and therefore to be avoided by predators looking for a light snack. The moth, which can often be seen flying during the day, is very variable, and so is the caterpillar, which has the same colouring as the adult.

caterpillar

GEOMETRIDAE (GEOMETER MOTHS)

March Moth
Alsophila aescularia

ID FACT FILE

WINGSPAN:
2.5–3.5 cm

DESCRIPTION:
Males are mostly
grey-brown, with
a whitish zig-zag
line running
across the
forewings.
Females are
darker and have
no wings

**HIBERNATING
STAGE:**
Pupa

FLIGHT PERIOD:
Early spring

**CATERPILLAR FOOD
PLANTS:**
Many deciduous
trees and shrubs

This is a common moth in most of central
Europe and the British Isles. It is unusual in
that the female is completely wingless, making
it look rather spidery. It can be found almost
anywhere that trees grow, and is sometimes a
pest in orchards. The caterpillar is yellowish-
green, striped with white lines, and can be dis-
tinguished from other looper moth caterpillars
as it has three pairs of prolegs instead of the
usual two.

female

male

GEOMETRIDAE (GEOMETER MOTHS)

J F M A M J
J A S O N D

Peppered Moth
Biston betularia

ID FACT FILE

WINGSPAN:
3.5–6 cm

DESCRIPTION:
Heavy grey-brown
speckling on a
whitish ground
colour. Male and
female very
similar

**HIBERNATING
STAGE:**
Pupa

FLIGHT PERIOD:
Late spring to
early summer

**CATERPILLAR FOOD
PLANTS:**
Most deciduous
trees and shrubs

This moth is very famous because during the
late 19th century and early 20th century, an
hereditary black form became more common
as it survived better in grimy, heavily industri-
alised areas. It is very common throughout
most of Europe, seen usually in open woodland, parks and gardens. The amazingly twig-
like caterpillar can be either green or brown in
colour, and has a number of warts to complete
the illusion of a small jointed twig.

caterpillar

normal and black forms

GEOMETRIDAE (GEOMETER MOTHS)

Yellow Shell
Camptogramma bilineata

ID FACT FILE

WINGSPAN:
2–2.5 cm

DESCRIPTION:
Yellow to dark
yellow-brown
wings and body
with fine lines in
slightly darker
shade. A wide
band of darker
yellow runs
through the
middle of each
wing. Sexes alike

**HIBERNATING
STAGE:**
Caterpillar

FLIGHT PERIOD:
Early to
mid-summer

**CATERPILLAR FOOD
PLANTS:**
Many low-growing
plants e.g. nettle
(*Urtica*)

This is a very variable and very common moth,
found throughout Europe, with many forms
and several named sub-species. It is possible to
find the moth through most of the summer in
almost any situation, wherever the food plants
grow. The caterpillar may be either green or
brown and, when at rest, curls the head under
the body. When fully grown, it will burrow
underground and make a silk cocoon in which
to pupate.

caterpillar

GEOMETRIDAE (GEOMETER MOTHS)

J	F	M	A	M	J
J	A	S	O	N	D

Barred Yellow
Cidaria fulvata

ID FACT FILE

WINGSPAN:
2–2.5 cm

DESCRIPTION:
Forewings yellow-brown with an uneven darker band through the middle and a paler triangular shape at the tips. Hindwings creamy white with yellowish border. Sexes alike

HIBERNATING STAGE:
Egg

FLIGHT PERIOD:
Summer

CATERPILLAR FOOD PLANTS:
Dog rose (*Rosa*), but in captivity will accept cultivated roses

This moth, common throughout most of Europe except the far north, can be seen flying on summer evenings almost as soon as the light begins to fade. During the day it hides under leaves and can be found mainly in hedgerows and other areas of low scrub, wherever the food plants can find support to grow. The very flimsy cocoon is made in amongst the leaves, and the moth emerges usually within a month.

caterpillar

Netted Pug
Eupithecia venosata

ID FACT FILE

WINGSPAN:
1.7–2.2 cm

DESCRIPTION:
Ground colour
white to yellow-
brown or grey
with dark brown
or black spider's-
web pattern.
Sexes alike

**HIBERNATING
STAGE:**
Pupa

FLIGHT PERIOD:
Late spring

**CATERPILLAR FOOD
PLANTS:**
Various species
of campion
(*Silene*)

Widespread throughout Europe, this little
moth can be found almost anywhere, from
lowlands to mountains, that the food plants will
grow. The adults show considerable variation,
especially in the ground colour of the wings,
and this seems to be geographically deter-
mined. The caterpillar lives inside the seed-
heads of its food plants, but when fully grown
at the end of summer it will leave this shelter
and burrow underground to pupate in a small
chamber.

caterpillar

Large Emerald
Geometra papilionaria

ID FACT FILE

WINGSPAN:
4–5 cm

DESCRIPTION:
Pale emerald-green with 2 rows of paler spots across each wing. Sexes alike

HIBERNATING STAGE:
Caterpillar

FLIGHT PERIOD:
Mid-summer

CATERPILLAR FOOD PLANTS:
Birch (*Betula*), alder (*Alnus*), beech (*Fagus*) and hazel (*Corylus*)

This attractive moth is common throughout most of Europe, and can be found in open deciduous woodlands, hedgerows, moorland and fenland areas, right up into the mountains. The green colour fades a little as the moth ages. The caterpillar remains brown through the winter while it hibernates on a twig, changing colour in the spring as the plants begin to grow again. When fully grown it pupates in a cocoon made amongst leaf-litter.

caterpillar

J	F	M	A	M	J
J	A	S	O	N	D

Common Emerald
Hemithea aestivaria

ID FACT FILE

WINGSPAN:
2.4–2.7 cm

DESCRIPTION:
Very pale green with a slightly darker band edged with white running through the middle of each wing. Slight suggestion of tails on the hind-wings. Sexes alike

HIBERNATING STAGE:
Caterpillar

FLIGHT PERIOD:
Early to mid-summer

CATERPILLAR FOOD PLANTS:
Various low-growing plants in autumn, deciduous trees and shrubs in spring

Although perhaps not quite as widespread as its name might suggest, this moth can be found in and around deciduous woodland through most of central and S Europe, becoming much rarer further north. The caterpillar is rather unusual because after hibernation it complete-ly changes the kind of plant that it feeds on. When fully grown it pupates in a flimsy cocoon in amongst the leaves of its food plant.

caterpillar

GEOMETRIDAE (GEOMETER MOTHS)

J	F	M	A	M	J
J	A	S	O	N	D

Brindled Beauty
Lycia hirtaria

ID FACT FILE

WINGSPAN:
3.5–4.5 cm

DESCRIPTION:
Furry-looking, mainly pale peppery grey-brown, with darker bands across the forewings. Female much paler; male has very feathery antennae and a distinct thin pale band close to the edge of the forewings

HIBERNATING STAGE:
Pupa

FLIGHT PERIOD:
Spring

CATERPILLAR FOOD PLANTS:
Most deciduous trees

This common moth can be found throughout most of Europe, wherever deciduous trees grow: woodlands, parks, gardens and orchards. The twig-like caterpillar, which can sometimes be a minor pest of apple trees, varies in colour from grey to reddish-brown, with darker markings and yellow spots around the middle segments. In autumn it burrows underground at the base of the tree to make a small chamber for pupation.

female

male

GEOMETRIDAE (GEOMETER MOTHS)

J	F	M	A	M	J
J	A	S	O	N	D

Chimney Sweeper
Odezia atrata

ID FACT FILE

WINGSPAN:
2.3–2.7 cm

DESCRIPTION:
Completely black
with just a thin
white edge at the
tips of the
forewings. Sexes
alike

HIBERNATING STAGE:
Egg

FLIGHT PERIOD:
Early summer

CATERPILLAR FOOD PLANTS:
Pignut
(*Conopodium*),
and related
plants

Although widespread through much of central
and N Europe, this little moth is found only in
small communities, usually in damp, grassy
places; but wherever it is seen, it is normally
fairly common. The moth flies during the day
amongst low-growing flowers in sunny places,
and there are often several flying in the same
area. The caterpillar usually feeds on the flowers of the food plant, and when fully grown
pupates underground.

caterpillar

GEOMETRIDAE (GEOMETER MOTHS)

J	F	M	A	M	J
J	A	S	O	N	D

Scalloped Hazel
Odontoptera bidentata

ID FACT FILE

WINGSPAN:
3.2–4 cm

DESCRIPTION:
Variable, but
usually pale
brown with a
slightly darker
black-edged band
across each
wing, each band
having a small
black oval ring in
the middle.
Forewings
strongly scal-
loped. Sexes
alike

**HIBERNATING
STAGE:**
Pupa

FLIGHT PERIOD:
Early summer

**CATERPILLAR FOOD
PLANTS:**
Most deciduous
trees

LOOKALIKES:
Early Thorn
(p.169)

This moth of woodlands and hedgerows is
common throughout most of Europe. It varies
quite a lot in colour and pattern. The caterpillar, too, varies in colour, from green to brown,
and one form is even speckled to match
lichens. In late summer, when the time comes
to pupate, the caterpillar will move down to
the trunk of whichever tree it has been feeding
on, and burrow under any moss growing on
the bark.

caterpillar

GEOMETRIDAE (GEOMETER MOTHS)

J	F	M	A	M	J
J	A	S	O	N	D

Brimstone Moth
Opisthograptis luteolata

ID FACT FILE

WINGSPAN:
3.2–3.7 cm

DESCRIPTION:
Distinctive bright yellow with tan markings and a small transparent crescent near the leading edge of the forewings. Sexes alike

HIBERNATING STAGE:
Pupa

FLIGHT PERIOD:
Spring to late summer

CATERPILLAR FOOD PLANTS:
Many deciduous shrubs and trees, particularly hawthorn (*Crataegus*) and sloe (*Prunus*)

This is a very common moth throughout Europe, frequently seen in towns where it is easily attracted to lights. Favoured habitats are hedgerows and open countryside, but it is becoming increasingly adapted to parks and gardens. The twig-like caterpillar may be either green or brown, and makes a cocoon near the ground in which to pupate. Since the two broods overlap, the moths seem to be on the wing for a long time.

caterpillar

GEOMETRIDAE (GEOMETER MOTHS)

J	F	M	A	M	J
J	A	S	O	N	D

Swallow-tailed Moth
Ourapteryx sambucaria

ID FACT FILE

WINGSPAN:
4–5 cm

DESCRIPTION:
Very pale creamy
yellow with 2 thin
pale brown lines
banding the
forewings and
1 line on the
hindwings, which
have short
triangular tails.
Sexes alike

**HIBERNATING
STAGE:**
Caterpillar

FLIGHT PERIOD:
Mid-summer

**CATERPILLAR FOOD
PLANTS:**
Many trees and
shrubs, particu-
larly ivy (*Hedera*),
privet (*Ligustrum*)
and hawthorn
(*Crataegus*)

One of the largest geometer moths to be found
in Europe, this species is common almost
everywhere except in the colder far north.
Normally to be seen in woodland areas, parks
and gardens, it is quite unmistakable when
seen at night; the flight is fast, yet fluttering,
and the colouring makes it easy to see. The
fully grown caterpillar pupates in early summer
in a thin cocoon suspended from a twig.

caterpillar

GEOMETRIDAE (GEOMETER MOTHS)

Early Thorn
Selenia dentaria

ID FACT FILE

WINGSPAN:
2.8–4 cm

DESCRIPTION:
Pale speckled brown with darker brown bands across the wings, less distinct on the hind wings. Each wing has a small transparent crescent. Females are slightly paler, and second generation adults are usually a little smaller

HIBERNATING STAGE:
Pupa

FLIGHT PERIOD:
Mid-spring and mid-summer: usually 2 broods, 1 in far north

CATERPILLAR FOOD PLANTS:
Many deciduous trees and shrubs

LOOKALIKES:
Scalloped Hazel (p.166)

This is a common moth throughout Europe, found in open woodland, hedgerows, parks and gardens. At rest the moth closes its wings in typical butterfly fashion and looks very much like a dead leaf. The twig-like caterpillar has two pairs of small humps on the lower back and varies in colour from reddish-brown to a darker, more chocolaty colour. Except in the far north, there are usually two broods each year.

caterpillar

GEOMETRIDAE (GEOMETER MOTHS)

Blood Vein
Timandra griseata

ID FACT FILE

WINGSPAN:
2.3–2.8 cm

DESCRIPTION:
Very pale pinkish-brown with a light reddish-brown line diagonally crossing the wings. When resting this looks like a straight line. Hindwings are drawn out to tiny points like tails. Sexes alike

HIBERNATING STAGE:
Caterpillar

FLIGHT PERIOD:
Early summer to autumn

CATERPILLAR FOOD PLANTS:
Low-growing plants such as sorrel (*Rumex*) and knotgrass (*Polygonum*)

An easily recognised moth of grassland, wasteland and hedgerows, this species is common throughout most of Europe, becoming more local further north. Depending on climate and locality, there may be one or two broods each year, and as a result the adults can be seen at varying times of the year; in England, for example, this is usually in June. The fully grown caterpillar pupates in a cocoon in amongst the leaves of the food plant.

caterpillar

GEOMETRIDAE (GEOMETER MOTHS)

J	F	M	A	M	J
J	A	S	O	N	D

Garden Carpet
Xanthorhoe fluctuata

ID FACT FILE

WINGSPAN:
1.8–2.5 cm

DESCRIPTION:
White to darkish grey with many fine wavy lines running across the wings. Along the leading edge of the forewings are 3 much darker patches, the largest in the middle

HIBERNATING STAGE:
Pupa

FLIGHT PERIOD:
Late spring to early autumn

CATERPILLAR FOOD PLANTS:
Wallflowers (*Cheiranthus*), cabbage (*Brassica*) and other Cruciferae, also currant (*Ribes*) bushes

This is probably one of the commonest of the European moths, being found almost everywhere, often in great numbers. There are two broods each year, sometimes more, and the moth seems to be on the wing for most of spring and summer, and is easily attracted to lights. The caterpillar varies in colour from pale green to grey and, when fully grown, burrows underground to make a cocoon in which to pupate.

caterpillar

LASIOCAMPIDAE (EGGARS)

J	F	M	A	M	J
J	A	S	O	N	D

Pine-tree Lappet
Dendrolimus pini

ID FACT FILE

WINGSPAN:
4.5–7 cm

DESCRIPTION:
Very variable.
Males usually
rich light reddish-
brown with 2
bands of pale
brown on the
forewings and a
white spot in the
middle of each
wing. Hindwings
are plain.
Females much
larger and paler,
rarely seen

**HIBERNATING
STAGE:**
Caterpillar

FLIGHT PERIOD:
Summer

**CATERPILLAR FOOD
PLANTS:**
Pine (*Pinus*)
trees

This variable moth can be found throughout
most of Europe, but is absent from the British
Isles. As its name might suggest, it is normally
seen in pine forests and plantations, up to
around 1500 m. The caterpillar is pale brown
with a darker pattern along the back and covered with short hairs. In colder regions they
can sometimes take two years to develop,
hibernating through two winters. In the south
they are often regarded as a pest.

male

left female
right male

LASIOCAMPIDAE (EGGARS)

Lappet
Gastropacha quercifolia

ID FACT FILE

WINGSPAN:
5–9 cm

DESCRIPTION:
Ground colour
usually rich
reddish-brown
but this may
vary. Edges of
the wings
scalloped. At
rest the moth
looks like a
bunch of dead
beech leaves.
Sexes alike, but
female larger

**HIBERNATING
STAGE:**
Caterpillar

FLIGHT PERIOD:
Summer

**CATERPILLAR FOOD
PLANTS:**
A number of
trees and shrubs
including fruit
trees, but partic-
ularly sloe
(*Prunus*) and
hawthorn
(*Crataegus*)

A beautiful, well-camouflaged moth, becoming
rarer owing to pesticides, although it can still
be found throughout most of Europe except
Ireland, Scotland and N Scandinavia. The
name comes from the fleshy 'lappets' down the
sides of the caterpillar which help to conceal it
by reducing shadow. The caterpillar spends the
winter on a twig while still small, then when
fully grown it makes a cocoon attached to a
branch in which to pupate.

caterpillar

J	F	M	A	M	J
J	A	S	O	N	D

Oak Eggar
Lasiocampa quercus

ID FACT FILE

WINGSPAN:
4.5–7.5 cm

DESCRIPTION:
Middle two-thirds
of each wing on
male is dark
brown with a
white central
spot. Remaining
third is pale
radiating out-
wards to darker
brown. Female
much larger and
paler

**HIBERNATING
STAGE:**
Caterpillar

FLIGHT PERIOD:
Summer

**CATERPILLAR FOOD
PLANTS:**
Bramble (*Rubus*)
and many trees
and shrubs

A moth of open woodland, heaths and grassland up to around 1500 m, and common
throughout Europe except the far north. The
male can often be seen flying on a sunny day,
but the female normally does not move until
late afternoon. The dark brown caterpillar has
black rings that are visible only when it curls
up, a broken white stripe along each side, and
is covered with short hairs.

female

male

LASIOCAMPIDAE (EGGARS)

J	F	M	A	M	J
J	A	S	O	N	D

Lackey
Malacosoma neustria

ID FACT FILE

WINGSPAN:
2.5–3.5 cm

DESCRIPTION:
Males very pale, cream to light brown, slightly darker towards outer edges of forewings and with 2 fine dark lines across the middle. Females larger and slightly darker, the 2 lines replaced by a broad band

HIBERNATING STAGE:
Egg

FLIGHT PERIOD:
Summer

CATERPILLAR FOOD PLANTS:
Hawthorn (*Crataegus*), sloe (*Prunus*) and a variety of deciduous trees

This is a common moth throughout most of Europe except Scotland and the far north. It can be seen in woodlands, gardens and orchards, wherever suitable trees and shrubs are growing. Caterpillars are gregarious, living in a silken 'tent' made amongst the leaves of the food plant. The caterpillar is greyish-blue, striped along the back in black, red and white, and covered in short hairs. The cocoon contains a yellow powder which may irritate sensitive skin.

female

male

LASIOCAMPIDAE (EGGARS)

J	F	M	A	M	J
J	A	S	O	N	D

Drinker

Philudoria potatoria

ID FACT FILE

WINGSPAN:
4.5–6.5 cm

DESCRIPTION:
Males are light orange-brown with a thin diagonal line on the forewings and 2 white spots. Females are larger and much paler

HIBERNATING STAGE:
Caterpillar

FLIGHT PERIOD:
Summer

CATERPILLAR FOOD PLANTS:
Various coarse grasses

This moth is fairly common throughout Europe, and prefers damp grassland, moorland and fens up to around 1500 m. The odd name comes from the caterpillar's habit of drinking droplets of water. The caterpillar is dark grey with two lines of tiny yellow dots along its back, and many small tufts of black hair. There are also tufts of white hair in a row along the sides.

male

female

SATURNIIDAE (SILK MOTHS)

J	F	M	A	M	J
J	A	S	O	N	D

Tau Emperor
Aglia tau

ID FACT FILE

WINGSPAN:
6.3–8.5 cm

DESCRIPTION:
Dark sand-coloured wings with a wavy black line near the edges. Large eye-spot in the middle of each wing with a white 'I'. Female larger and paler

HIBERNATING STAGE:
Pupa

FLIGHT PERIOD:
Spring

CATERPILLAR FOOD PLANTS:
Beech (*Fagus*), oak (*Quercus*) and many other trees

This moth is fairly common throughout most of central Europe, and although absent from the British Isles it is found as far north as S Scandinavia and as far south as N Spain. It prefers deciduous woodland up to around 1600 m, the male flying during the afternoon, the female at night. The young caterpillar has several reddish spines which it loses about halfway through its development. It pupates on the ground in a cocoon.

male

caterpillar

SATURNIIDAE (SILK MOTHS)

J	F	M	A	M	J
J	A	S	O	N	D

Emperor
Saturnia pavonia

ID FACT FILE

WINGSPAN:
4.8–8 cm

DESCRIPTION:
Male forewings
greyish-brown,
hindwings
orange-brown,
with large eye-
spot in each
wing. Female
larger, pale grey

**HIBERNATING
STAGE:**
Pupa

FLIGHT PERIOD:
Spring

**CATERPILLAR FOOD
PLANTS:**
Bramble (*Rubus*),
heather (*Erica*)
and other shrubs

This common moth is found right across
Europe, and prefers heaths and other
grasslands and open woodland, up to around
2000 m. The males can often be seen flying
during the day while they seek out a mate, but
females fly only at night. The caterpillar is black
at first, but soon changes to green, banded
black with yellow or red hairy warts. It pupates
in a tough, bottle-shaped cocoon with a carefully constructed
entrance to keep
out predators.

male

female

SATURNIIDAE (SILK MOTHS)

J	F	M	A	M	J
J	A	S	O	N	D

Great Peacock
Saturnia pyri

ID FACT FILE

WINGSPAN:
10–13 cm

DESCRIPTION:
Grey and greyish-brown edged with white and yellow, with a large eye-spot in the middle of each wing. Female larger

HIBERNATING STAGE:
Pupa

FLIGHT PERIOD:
Spring

CATERPILLAR FOOD PLANTS:
Mainly various fruit trees

This is the largest of any butterfly or moth species to be found in Europe, and is fairly common across the southern part of the continent. It prefers open countryside and is often seen around orchards, where the moths will sit on tree trunks during the day. The caterpillar is black at first, later changing to green with a yellow line along the sides and rows of hairy, bright blue warts. It pupates in a tough, pear-shaped cocoon, usually in a tree.

caterpillar

ENDROMIDAE

Kentish Glory
Endromis versicolora

ID FACT FILE

WINGSPAN:
5.7–8.3 cm

DESCRIPTION:
Dark brown forewings, orange-brown hindwings, marked with darker brown and white. Female has white hind-wings and is generally paler

HIBERNATING STAGE:
Pupa

FLIGHT PERIOD:
Early to mid-spring

CATERPILLAR FOOD PLANTS:
Birch (*Betula*) and a few other trees

This moth is locally common throughout most of central and N Europe, and also found in some southern parts where it is mainly restricted to the mountains up to around 2000 m. In the British Isles it is found only in Scotland (not – as the name might suggest – in Kent!) It prefers open woodland and heaths, and males can often be seen flying during the day. The caterpillar is black at first, changing to green later, and pupates in a rough cocoon on the ground.

male

caterpillar

SPHINGIDAE (HAWKMOTHS)

J	F	M	A	M	J
J	A	S	O	N	D

Elephant Hawkmoth
Deilephila elpenor

ID FACT FILE

WINGSPAN:
5.8–7 cm

DESCRIPTION:
Deep pink with bands of olive-green; hindwings marked with black near body. Legs and antennae white. Female larger

HIBERNATING STAGE:
Pupa

FLIGHT PERIOD:
Early summer

CATERPILLAR FOOD PLANTS:
Willowherb (*Epilobium*); fuchsia in gardens

LOOKALIKES:
Small Elephant Hawkmoth (p.182)

This moth is common throughout Europe, preferring open woodland, waste ground, parks and gardens in lowland areas, wherever the food plant grows. The odd name describes the caterpillar, which has a tapering front end that looks slightly like an elephant's trunk. This can be withdrawn rapidly to puff up the alarming false eye-spots. Caterpillars are often seen in August moving quickly across open ground as they look for somewhere to pupate.

caterpillar

| J | F | M | A | M | J |
| J | A | S | O | N | D |

SPHINGIDAE (HAWKMOTHS)

Small Elephant Hawkmoth

Deilephila porcellus

ID FACT FILE

WINGSPAN:
4.3–5.2 cm

DESCRIPTION:
Similar to the
Elephant Hawk-
moth but small-
er, and with no
black on the
hindwings. Green
markings are
more yellowish

**HIBERNATING
STAGE:**
Pupa

FLIGHT PERIOD:
Late spring

**CATERPILLAR FOOD
PLANTS:**
Bedstraw
(*Galium*) and
willowherb
(*Epilobium*)

LOOKALIKES:
Elephant Hawk-
moth (p.181)

This moth is common throughout most of
Europe except N Scandinavia and Finland. It
prefers heaths, meadows and other open grasslands, and is strongly attracted to honeysuckle
(*Lonicera*) flowers. The caterpillar may be
either green or brown, and although it is similar to the Elephant Hawkmoth caterpillar, it is
smaller and has no horn at the tail end. It
pupates on the ground in a loose cocoon
amongst leaf-litter.

caterpillar

SPHINGIDAE (HAWKMOTHS)

Broad-bordered Bee Hawkmoth

Hemaris fuciformis

J	F	M	A	M	J
J	A	S	O	N	D

ID FACT FILE

WINGSPAN:
4.2–5 cm

DESCRIPTION:
Wings transparent with brown edges; body pale greenish-brown with a dark brown band, white at the sides. Sexes alike

HIBERNATING STAGE:
Pupa

FLIGHT PERIOD:
Late spring to early summer

CATERPILLAR FOOD PLANTS:
Honeysuckle (*Lonicera*) and bedstraw (*Galium*)

This moth is fairly common throughout most of Europe except the far north and parts of Spain. In the British Isles it is found only in S England and Wales. It prefers open woodlands and forest edges, also flowery meadows up to around 2000 m. It flies during the day and looks amazingly like a bee, except that it can fly much faster. The fully grown caterpillar pupates on the ground in a loose cocoon amongst dead leaves.

grey scales on wings fall off during 1st flight

caterpillar

SPHINGIDAE (HAWKMOTHS)

J	F	M	A	M	J
J	A	S	O	N	D

Spurge Hawkmoth
Hyles euphorbiae

ID FACT FILE

WINGSPAN:
5.5–7 cm

DESCRIPTION:
Forewings
patterned in
mid-brown and
dark cream, hind-
wings dark
brown, cream
and pink. Legs
and antennae
cream. Sexes
alike

**HIBERNATING
STAGE:**
Pupa

FLIGHT PERIOD:
Late spring and
late summer

**CATERPILLAR FOOD
PLANTS:**
Spurge
(*Euphorbia*)

This moth is common across central and S
Europe, but migrates northwards each year,
sometimes reaching as far as S England. It
prefers waste ground and open grassland,
wherever the food plants grow. There are
usually two broods each year. The brightly
coloured caterpillar is poisonous (i.e. tastes
nasty) and does not have to hide; when fully
grown it pupates in a flimsy cocoon just under
the surface of loose soil.

caterpillar

SPHINGIDAE (HAWKMOTHS)

J	F	M	A	M	J
J	A	S	O	N	D

Hyles vespertilio

ID FACT FILE

WINGSPAN:
6–7.5 cm

DESCRIPTION:
Forewings and
body bluish-grey;
hindwings pink,
edged black.
Sexes alike

**HIBERNATING
STAGE:**
Pupa

FLIGHT PERIOD:
Late spring and
late summer

**CATERPILLAR FOOD
PLANTS:**
Willowherb
(*Epilobium*) and
bedstraw
(*Galium*)

This moth is fairly common in most parts of
S Europe except Spain, but it is not a migratory species, and is rarely found further north.
It prefers dry, open grassland, including mountain pastures, wherever the food plants grow.
There is normally only one brood each year,
with a partial second brood in very warm summers. The caterpillar feeds mainly at night,
hiding during the day at the base of the plant,
sometimes even under stones on the ground.
When fully grown it pupates in a flimsy cocoon
amongst leaf-litter.

caterpillar

SPHINGIDAE (HAWKMOTHS)

J	F	M	A	M	J
J	A	S	O	N	D

Pine Hawkmoth
Hyloicus pinastri

ID FACT FILE

WINGSPAN:
7–9 cm

DESCRIPTION:
Forewings soft
grey with darker
markings,
hindwings
brownish-grey,
lighter near the
body. Sexes
alike

**HIBERNATING
STAGE:**
Pupa

FLIGHT PERIOD:
Early summer

**CATERPILLAR FOOD
PLANTS:**
Pine (*Pinus*) and
spruce (*Picea*)

This moth is fairly common throughout most of
Europe, except Scotland and Ireland. It is
restricted to pine forests, mainly in lowland
areas, where it can sometimes be seen sitting
on a tree trunk during the day. At night it is
attracted to flowers such as honeysuckle
(*Lonicera*). The caterpillar is well camouflaged,
and when fully grown it pupates underground,
often wandering a long way from the food
plant first.

caterpillar

SPHINGIDAE (HAWKMOTHS)

J	F	M	A	M	J
J	A	S	O	N	D

Poplar Hawkmoth
Laothoe populi

ID FACT FILE

WINGSPAN:
7–9 cm

DESCRIPTION:
Marbled shades
of light and dark
grey. Hindwings
have a reddish-
brown patch near
the body. Female
larger

**HIBERNATING
STAGE:**
Pupa

FLIGHT PERIOD:
Late spring, also
late summer in
the south

**CATERPILLAR FOOD
PLANTS:**
Poplar (*Populus*),
sallow and willow
(*Salix*)

This moth is very common throughout Europe,
although perhaps less so in the south. It
prefers open woodland, parks and gardens,
mainly in damp lowland areas. The adults do
not feed, but are easily attracted to lights.
There are usually two broods each year in the
south, but only one further north. The caterpillar is very well camouflaged, and when fully
grown it pupates underground in a small
chamber.

male

caterpillar

SPHINGIDAE (HAWKMOTHS)

Hummingbird Hawkmoth

Macroglossum stellatarum

ID FACT FILE

WINGSPAN:
4–5 cm

DESCRIPTION:
Forewings grey with darker wavy lines; hindwings light orange-brown. Tail of body black and white. Sexes alike

HIBERNATING STAGE:
Adult, sometimes pupa. Can only survive in the south

FLIGHT PERIOD:
All year

CATERPILLAR FOOD PLANTS:
Bedstraw (*Galium*) and valerian (*Centranthus*)

This moth is very common in S Europe, but migrates northwards every year, reaching as far as N Scandinavia and the British Isles. It can be found almost anywhere, but especially in parks and gardens. It flies during the day, and if it finds a well-stocked garden, it will stay for several days, patrolling regularly every four hours. There are two broods each year in S Europe, but adults may be seen all year. The fully grown caterpillar pupates in a flimsy cocoon on the ground amongst leaf-litter.

caterpillar

SPHINGIDAE (HAWKMOTHS)

J	F	M	A	M	J
J	A	S	O	N	D

Oak Hawkmoth
Marumba quercus

ID FACT FILE

WINGSPAN:
9–11 cm

DESCRIPTION:
Forewings
banded with pale
shades of brown;
hindwings plain,
slightly more
orange. Female
much larger

**HIBERNATING
STAGE:**
Pupa

FLIGHT PERIOD:
Early summer

**CATERPILLAR FOOD
PLANTS:**
Oak (*Quercus*)

This very large moth is found only in
S Europe, mainly along the Mediterranean
coast, where it is common. It prefers low hillsides with open woodland, wherever the food
plant grows. As an adult, it does not feed, but
can sometimes be seen during the day sitting
on a tree trunk. The caterpillar thrives in sunlight, although it shelters under a leaf at all
times. When fully grown the caterpillar
changes to a reddish-brown colour before
pupating underground.

caterpillar

female

SPHINGIDAE (HAWKMOTHS)

Lime Hawkmoth
Mimas tiliae

ID FACT FILE

WINGSPAN:
6–8 cm

DESCRIPTION:
Variable: usually
pale brown,
sometimes
green; forewings
patterned with
darker green and
2 large dark
green spots.
Sexes alike

**HIBERNATING
STAGE:**
Pupa

FLIGHT PERIOD:
Late spring to
early summer

**CATERPILLAR FOOD
PLANTS:**
Lime (*Tilia*), elm
(*Ulmus*) and
alder (*Alnus*)

This moth is very common throughout most
of Europe except N Scandinavia, Scotland and
Ireland. It is a lowland species, preferring open
woodland, parks and gardens, even streets if
they are planted with lime trees. The adult
moth does not feed, but is easily attracted to
bright lights. When fully grown the caterpillar
changes to a pinkish-brown colour, and in
towns it can often be seen wandering across
pavements as it looks for somewhere to pupate.

caterpillar

SPHINGIDAE (HAWKMOTHS)

Eyed Hawkmoth
Smerinthus ocellata

J	F	M	A	M	J
J	A	S	O	N	D

ID FACT FILE

WINGSPAN:
7.6–9 cm

DESCRIPTION:
Forewings
marbled with
shades of brown;
hindwings pink
with a large blue
and black eye-
spot in the
middle of each.
Sexes alike

**HIBERNATING
STAGE:**
Pupa

FLIGHT PERIOD:
Late spring to
early summer

**CATERPILLAR FOOD
PLANTS:**
Sallow and willow
(*Salix*), poplar
(*Populus*) and
apple (*Malus*)

This moth is locally common throughout most
of Europe except Scotland and the far north. It
prefers open woodland, orchards, parks and
gardens up to around 1600 m. It does not feed
as an adult, but can sometimes be found sitting
on a tree trunk during the day. If it is disturbed
when resting it simply raises its forewings to
expose the false eye-spots on the hindwings.
The fully grown caterpillar pupates underground in a small chamber.

caterpillar

SPHINGIDAE (HAWKMOTHS)

Privet Hawkmoth

Sphinx ligustri

ID FACT FILE

WINGSPAN:
9–12 cm

DESCRIPTION:
Forewings pale
and dark brown
with black
streaks; hind-
wings banded in
pink and black.
Abdomen also
striped pink and
black. Sexes
alike

**HIBERNATING
STAGE:**
Pupa

FLIGHT PERIOD:
Early summer

**CATERPILLAR FOOD
PLANTS:**
Privet (*Ligustrum*),
lilac (*Syringa*)
and ash (*Fraxinus*)

This very large moth, common throughout
most of Europe but absent from Scotland and
Ireland, migrates northwards every year,
adding to resident colonies. It prefers open
woodland, shrubby hillsides, parks and
gardens, and can sometimes be seen flying
around flowers at night. When fully grown the
caterpillar turns brown along its back and may
wander a long way from its food plant before
burrowing underground to pupate.

caterpillar

NOTODONTIDAE (PROMINENT MOTHS)

Puss Moth
Cerura vinula

ID FACT FILE

WINGSPAN:
6–8 cm

DESCRIPTION:
Very hairy, white, with black spots and a pattern of wavy black lines. Veins picked out in yellow on forewings; brown on hindwings. Sexes alike

HIBERNATING STAGE:
Pupa

FLIGHT PERIOD:
Mid-spring to mid-summer

CATERPILLAR FOOD PLANTS:
Poplar (*Populus*), sallow and willow (*Salix*)

J	F	M	A	M	J
J	A	S	O	N	D

This moth is common almost everywhere in Europe, preferring open woodland and hedgerows up to around 2500 m. The name 'Puss' comes from the furry appearance of the adult, which is often attracted to bright lights at night. The amazing caterpillar changes to a rich plum colour just before pupating, and makes a rock-hard cocoon on the side of a tree, mixing bits of chewed bark in with the silk to disguise it.

caterpillar

NOTODONTIDAE (PROMINENT MOTHS)

J	F	M	A	M	J
J	A	S	O	N	D

Pebble Prominent
Eligmodonta ziczac

ID FACT FILE

WINGSPAN:
4.5–5 cm

DESCRIPTION:
Forewings
orange-brown
and grey with a
large, dark
brown, pebble-
like marking at
the tip; hind-
wings pale brown
with darker
edges. Sexes
alike

**HIBERNATING
STAGE:**
Pupa

FLIGHT PERIOD:
Late spring and
late summer

**CATERPILLAR FOOD
PLANTS:**
Sallow and willow
(*Salix*)

caterpillar

Found throughout Europe, this is a very
common moth, preferring damp woodland
edges and hedgerows, sometimes large parks
and similar areas, up to around 2500 m. In the
north and in the mountains there is only one
brood a year, but in the warmer south there
are usually two. The odd-looking caterpillar is
normally pale greyish-brown, but this may
vary. When fully grown it comes down from
the tree and burrows underground to pupate.

NOTODONTIDAE (PROMINENT MOTHS)

J	F	M	A	M	J
J	A	S	O	N	D

Iron Prominent
Notodonta dromedarius

ID FACT FILE

WINGSPAN:
4–5 cm

DESCRIPTION:
Forewings dark grey with rust-brown and cream markings, but colours may vary. Hindwings pale grey-brown. Sexes alike

HIBERNATING STAGE:
Pupa

FLIGHT PERIOD:
Late spring to mid-summer

CATERPILLAR FOOD PLANTS:
Birch (*Betula*) and alder (*Alnus*)

This moth is fairly common throughout northern and central Europe, preferring open woodland and large parks, where the main food trees grow. The grey colouring of the wings matches the bark of birch trees very well, and makes the moth almost invisible. The caterpillar, which may vary in colour from green to brown, is easily recognised by the four humps on its back. It pupates in a cocoon at the base of the tree.

caterpillar

NOTODONTIDAE (PROMINENT MOTHS)

J	F	M	A	M	J
J	A	S	O	N	D

Buff Tip
Phalera bucephalus

ID FACT FILE

WINGSPAN:
5–6.5 cm

DESCRIPTION:
Forewings
shades of grey
patterned with
black and brown
and with a
yellowish patch
at the tips; hind-
wings creamy
white. Sexes
alike

**HIBERNATING
STAGE:**
Pupa

FLIGHT PERIOD:
Late spring to
mid-summer

**CATERPILLAR FOOD
PLANTS:**
Mainly oak
(*Quercus*), but
also other
deciduous trees

This moth is very common throughout Europe,
found in deciduous woodland and also parks
and gardens. It wraps its wings tightly around
its body when resting during the day and looks
amazingly like a broken twig, making it very
hard to spot. The brightly coloured caterpillars
live together in a group when young,
completely stripping the leaves from whole
branches, but they separate when nearly fully
grown. Pupation takes place underground.

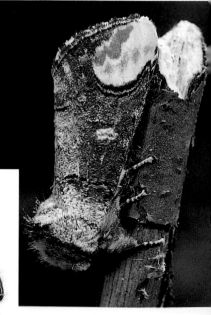

caterpillar

J	F	M	A	M	J
J	A	S	O	N	D

Swallow Prominent
Pheosia tremula

ID FACT FILE

WINGSPAN:
5–6 cm

DESCRIPTION:
Forewings very pale grey edged with dark brown and a yellowish triangular patch near the body; hindwings white, dark brown at the bottom edge. Sexes alike

HIBERNATING STAGE:
Pupa

FLIGHT PERIOD:
Late spring and mid-summer

CATERPILLAR FOOD PLANTS:
Poplar (*Populus*) and willow (*Salix*)

This moth is common throughout Europe, found mainly in the lowlands in open woodland and surrounding areas. It is very well camouflaged and hard to spot when resting on a tree trunk during the day. There are usually two broods each year, though only one in the far north. The caterpillar, which is usually green, sometimes brown, burrows underground if it is to pupate over winter; otherwise it makes a cocoon amongst the leaves.

caterpillar

NOTODONTIDAE (PROMINENT MOTHS)

J	F	M	A	M	J
J	A	S	O	N	D

Coxcomb Prominent
Ptilodon capucina

ID FACT FILE

WINGSPAN:
3.5–4.3 cm

DESCRIPTION:
Forewings rich reddish-brown with a slightly darker band across the middle. Hindwings very pale brown, darker at the bottom edges. Sexes alike

HIBERNATING STAGE:
Pupa

FLIGHT PERIOD:
Late spring and late summer

CATERPILLAR FOOD PLANTS:
Poplar (*Populus*), birch (*Betula*) and other trees and shrubs

This very common moth is found throughout Europe in deciduous woodlands and hedgerows, and also parks and gardens. It looks very much like a dead leaf and is not easily spotted. At night it can be attracted to bright lights. There are two broods each year. The caterpillar varies in colour from green to shades of brown, but always has two small bright red projections at the tail end. When fully grown it pupates underground at the base of a tree.

caterpillar

NOTODONTIDAE (PROMINENT MOTHS)

Lobster Moth
Stauropus fagi

J	F	M	A	M	J
J	A	S	O	N	D

ID FACT FILE

WINGSPAN:
5.5–7 cm

DESCRIPTION:
Very hairy,
generally pale
greyish-brown;
forewings pat-
terned with dark
spots and wavy
whitish lines.
Sexes alike

**HIBERNATING
STAGE:**
Pupa

FLIGHT PERIOD:
Late spring to
mid-summer

**CATERPILLAR FOOD
PLANTS:**
Mainly beech
(*Fagus*), also
birch (*Betula*)
and oak
(*Quercus*)

This moth is not very common, but is found
throughout Europe except the far north. In the
British Isles it occurs only in southern parts of
England, Wales and Ireland. It is very much a
woodland species. The newly hatched
caterpillars are black and look a little like ants
or spiders, but when they are fully grown they
look very peculiar, and can spit acid if
disturbed. They pupate in a cocoon made
between two leaves.

caterpillar

NOCTUIDAE (OWLET MOTHS)

J	F	M	A	M	J
J	A	S	O	N	D

Alder Moth
Acronicta alni

ID FACT FILE

WINGSPAN:
3.3–4 cm

DESCRIPTION:
Forewings pale grey with fine black markings and a black shadow-like patch. Hindwings white, grey at the edges. Sexes alike

HIBERNATING STAGE:
Pupa

FLIGHT PERIOD:
Late spring

CATERPILLAR FOOD PLANTS:
Alder (*Alnus*), oak (*Quercus*) and many other trees

A locally common moth, found in lowland deciduous woods and forests throughout Europe. The adult is not often seen as it blends so well with the tree bark on which it normally sits during the day. The young caterpillar looks very much like a bird-dropping, but when fully grown the striking black and yellow pattern makes it easier to spot. It usually pupates just under the bark of a tree.

caterpillar

NOCTUIDAE (OWLET MOTHS)

Green-brindled Crescent

Allophyes oxyacanthae

ID FACT FILE

WINGSPAN:
3.5–4.5 cm

DESCRIPTION:
Forewings have a green sheen overlaying pale brown with a broad dark grey band and a small white crescent-shaped mark. Hindwings pale brown. Sexes alike

HIBERNATING STAGE:
Egg

FLIGHT PERIOD:
Early autumn

CATERPILLAR FOOD PLANTS:
Sloe (*Prunus*), hawthorn (*Crataegus*) and apple (*Malus*)

This moth is common throughout Europe, preferring lowland forests, woods and hedgerows. The beautiful colouring can make it difficult to see during the day when at rest on a tree trunk, but at night it is strongly attracted to autumn flowers such as ivy (*Hedera*). When fully grown, the well-camouflaged caterpillar – easily recognised by two small pointed bumps at the tail end – makes a cocoon on the ground amongst leaf-litter in which to pupate.

caterpillar

Beautiful Yellow Underwing

Anarta myrtilli

J	F	M	A	M	J
J	A	S	O	N	D

ID FACT FILE

WINGSPAN:
2–2.5 cm

DESCRIPTION:
Forewings mottled with reddish-brown and black on white, hindwings bright yellow with a broad black border. Sexes alike

HIBERNATING STAGE:
Pupa

FLIGHT PERIOD:
Late spring to mid-summer, depending on broods and locality

CATERPILLAR FOOD PLANTS:
Ling (*Calluna*) and heather (*Erica*)

This little moth is common throughout Europe, found mainly in heathland and moorland, everywhere the food plant grows, up to around 2000 m. It flies only during sunny weather, hiding away on cloudy days. The caterpillar, too, is active mainly during the day, but is extremely well camouflaged and hard to spot. When fully grown it pupates in a cocoon on the ground amongst leaf-litter. There may be two broods each year, depending on locality.

caterpillar

NOCTUIDAE (OWLET MOTHS)

J	F	M	A	M	J
J	A	S	O	N	D

Silver Y
Autographa gamma

ID FACT FILE

WINGSPAN:
3.5–4.3 cm

DESCRIPTION:
Forewings light brownish-grey mottled with darker shades and marked with a silvery-white 'Y'. Hindwings pale brown. 2 prominent tufts of hair on the back. Sexes alike

HIBERNATING STAGE:
Caterpillar

FLIGHT PERIOD:
Late spring to autumn; 2 broods

CATERPILLAR FOOD PLANTS:
Many low-growing plants

This moth is mainly resident in S Europe, but migrates northwards every year; it can reach as far north as Lapland, but cannot survive the winter anywhere. It is found almost everywhere, having no strong preferences except a good supply of flowers. It can be seen flying during both day and night, but most particularly at dusk. The caterpillar varies in colour from light to dark green, and pupates in a cocoon amongst leaf-litter.

caterpillar

NOCTUIDAE (OWLET MOTHS)

Mother Shipton
Callistege mi

ID FACT FILE

WINGSPAN:
2.7–3.5 cm

DESCRIPTION:
Forewings
greyish-brown
and white with a
darker pattern
that looks a bit
like a witch's
face; hindwings
dark brown with
yellow spots.
Sexes alike

**HIBERNATING
STAGE:**
Pupa

FLIGHT PERIOD:
Late spring and
mid-summer, but
spring only in
colder areas

**CATERPILLAR FOOD
PLANTS:**
Clover (*Trifolium*)
and related
plants

This is a common moth throughout Europe
except for N Scandinavia, and can be found in
open woodland and grassland up to around
1700 m. It can be seen flying during the day,
when it is easily mistaken for a Skipper
butterfly, but it does not feed and therefore
is not attracted to flowers. The slim, pale
brown caterpillar is well camouflaged, and
when fully grown pupates in a cocoon made
amongst grass blades.

caterpillar

J	F	M	A	M	J
J	A	S	O	N	D

Clifden Nonpareil
Catocala fraxini

ID FACT FILE

WINGSPAN:
7.5–10 cm

DESCRIPTION:
Forewings very
pale brownish-
grey with darker
mottled pattern;
hindwings black
with a white
fringe and
banded with pale
lilac-blue. Sexes
alike

**HIBERNATING
STAGE:**
Egg

FLIGHT PERIOD:
Mid-summer

**CATERPILLAR FOOD
PLANTS:**
Poplar (*Populus*)
and other trees

This large moth is common over much of
northern and central Europe, although it is not
found in the British Isles. On the rare
occasions when it has been discovered in
England, this is almost certainly due to
migration. It prefers open, deciduous
woodland and can be very hard to spot when
resting on a tree trunk during the day. The
caterpillar makes a flimsy cocoon amongst leaf-
litter on the ground in which to pupate.

caterpillar

NOCTUIDAE (OWLET MOTHS)

J	F	M	A	M	J
J	A	S	O	N	D

Red Underwing
Catocala nupta

ID FACT FILE

WINGSPAN:
7–8 cm

DESCRIPTION:
Forewings light
grey-brown with a
darker mottled
pattern; hind-
wings banded
black and scarlet
with a white
fringe

**HIBERNATING
STAGE:**
Egg

FLIGHT PERIOD:
Late summer

**CATERPILLAR FOOD
PLANTS:**
Poplar (*Populus*)
and related trees

This moth is common throughout most of
Europe, but is absent from N Scandinavia,
Scotland and Ireland. It prefers open
woodland, parks and gardens and is extremely
hard to spot when resting on a tree trunk, but
at night it is strongly attracted to rotten fruit.
The caterpillar feeds only at night, and when
fully grown pupates in a cocoon either amongst
leaf-litter on the ground or under bark.

caterpillar

NOCTUIDAE (OWLET MOTHS)

Antler Moth
Cerapteryx graminis

ID FACT FILE

WINGSPAN:
2.8–3.5 cm

DESCRIPTION:
Forewings mid-brown with darker spots, veins clearly marked in creamy white; hindwings brown, paler closer to body. Female larger and paler

HIBERNATING STAGE:
Egg

FLIGHT PERIOD:
Summer

CATERPILLAR FOOD PLANTS:
Coarse grasses

A very common moth in northern and central Europe, preferring open grassland up to around 2000 m. It flies during the day as well as at night. The female drops her eggs in flight, as do many grass-feeding species; the resulting caterpillars can sometimes cause a great deal of damage. They feed mainly at night, and when fully grown pupate in a cocoon made amongst grass roots.

caterpillar

NOCTUIDAE (OWLET MOTHS)

J	F	M	A	M	J
J	A	S	O	N	D

Shark
Cucullia umbraticae

ID FACT FILE

WINGSPAN:
4.5–5.5 cm

DESCRIPTION:
Forewings very
pale brownish-
grey patterned
with thin black
lines; hindwings
white with veins
picked out in
light brown.
Female darker

**HIBERNATING
STAGE:**
Pupa

FLIGHT PERIOD:
Late spring to
early summer

**CATERPILLAR FOOD
PLANTS:**
Low-growing
plants such as
lettuce (*Lactuca*)

This moth is very common throughout Europe,
where it prefers rough, open places, parks and
gardens, wherever it can find suitable food
plants. It is very well camouflaged and difficult
to spot when resting during the day, but at
night it is strongly attracted to flowers such as
honeysuckle (*Lonicera*). The caterpillar eats
the flowers as well as leaves and pupates on the
food plant in a very loose, flimsy cocoon.

caterpillar

NOCTUIDAE (OWLET MOTHS)

J	F	M	A	M	J
J	A	S	O	N	D

Mullein
Cucullia verbasci

ID FACT FILE

WINGSPAN:
4.5–5.5 cm

DESCRIPTION:
Forewings pale
brown with a
darker pattern
around the
edges; hindwings
dark brown, paler
near the body. All
wings are scal-
loped, and the
head is hidden
under a pointed
tuft of hair.
Sexes alike

**HIBERNATING
STAGE:**
Pupa

FLIGHT PERIOD:
Mid-spring

**CATERPILLAR FOOD
PLANTS:**
Mulleins
(*Verbascum*)

This moth is fairly common throughout most
of Europe, but it is absent from N Scandinavia
and Scotland. It is found in rough, open places,
wasteland and gardens, wherever the food plants
grow, but is very difficult to spot. The bright
colours of the caterpillar may be a warning to
predators that it has an unpleasant taste, but as
the adult is so well camouflaged this could be a
bluff. Pupation takes place underground.

caterpillar

NOCTUIDAE (OWLET MOTHS)

J	F	M	A	M	J
J	A	S	O	N	D

Burnished Brass
Diachrysia chrysitis

ID FACT FILE

WINGSPAN:
3.5–4.2 cm

DESCRIPTION:
Forewings banded with light pinkish-brown and shining brassy yellow; hindwings pale brown. Sexes alike

HIBERNATING STAGE:
Caterpillar

FLIGHT PERIOD:
Late spring and late summer

CATERPILLAR FOOD PLANTS:
Nettle (*Urtica*) and related plants

A very common moth found throughout Europe in gardens, hedgerows, meadows and anywhere else the food plant grows. Although it flies mainly at night, it can sometimes be seen on the wing during the day, when it will even sit for a while in the sun. There are two broods each year, sometimes only one in colder areas, and the fully grown caterpillar pupates in a white cocoon amongst leaves on the food plant.

caterpillar

NOCTUIDAE (OWLET MOTHS)

J	F	M	A	M	J
J	A	S	O	N	D

Frosted Orange
Gortyna flavago

ID FACT FILE

WINGSPAN:
3.8–4.3 cm

DESCRIPTION:
Light yellow-brown with darker markings and a thick brown band along the edge of the forewings; hindwings creamy white. Female larger

HIBERNATING STAGE:
Egg

FLIGHT PERIOD:
Late summer to mid-autumn

CATERPILLAR FOOD PLANTS:
Thistles (*Cirsium, Carduus*) and burdock (*Arctium*); sometimes potato (*Solanum*) or tomato (*Lycopersicon*)

This common moth is found throughout most of Europe except for the far north. It prefers open areas such as waste ground and farming land, particularly near damp or marshy places, and can sometimes become a minor pest. The caterpillar spends its entire life feeding inside the thick, pulpy central stem of the food plant, and when fully grown in early summer, it will pupate close to the ground, inside this hollowed-out home.

caterpillar

NOCTUIDAE (OWLET MOTHS)

J	F	M	A	M	J
J	A	S	O	N	D

Snout
Hypena probosidalis

ID FACT FILE

WINGSPAN:
2.5–3.8 cm

DESCRIPTION:
Forewings pale
brown with dark-
er bands and a
row of tiny white
spots; hindwings
pale brown,
plain. Sexes
alike

**HIBERNATING
STAGE:**
Caterpillar

FLIGHT PERIOD:
Late spring and
late summer

**CATERPILLAR FOOD
PLANTS:**
Nettle (*Urtica*)
and related
plants

This easily recognised moth is very common
throughout Europe, and is found in waste
ground, hedgerows and gardens, wherever the
food plant grows. The elongated palpi that
produce the 'snout' help the moth to look more
like a dead leaf. It never travels far, and
produces either one or two broods each year,
depending on the locality and climate. When
fully grown the caterpillar makes a cocoon
amongst the leaves of the food plant in which
to pupate.

caterpillar

NOCTUIDAE (OWLET MOTHS)

J	F	M	A	M	J
J	A	S	O	N	D

Cabbage Moth
Mamestra brassicae

ID FACT FILE

WINGSPAN:
4–4.7 cm

DESCRIPTION:
Forewings grey
with a darker
mottled pattern
and two light
spots near the
middle; hind-
wings light grey.
Sexes alike

**HIBERNATING
STAGE:**
Pupa

FLIGHT PERIOD:
Late spring to
early autumn,
depending on
locality

**CATERPILLAR FOOD
PLANTS:**
Cabbage (*Brassica*) and many
other low-growing
plants

This moth is one of the commonest pests of
gardens and agricultural land, and is found
throughout Europe, mainly in lowland areas,
though sometimes also in the mountains. It can
also be seen in most other parts of the
countryside as well, as cabbage is not the only
plant the caterpillars will eat. There is only one
brood each year in colder areas, but there may
be two or three elsewhere. The caterpillar can
be either green or brown, and when fully
grown it pupates underground.

caterpillar

NOCTUIDAE (OWLET MOTHS)

J	F	M	A	M	J
J	A	S	O	N	D

Dot Moth
Melanchra persicariae

ID FACT FILE

WINGSPAN:
3.7–4.5 cm

DESCRIPTION:
Forewings dark
grey patterned
with black and a
white spot near
the middle; hind-
wings light grey,
paler near the
body. Sexes
alike

**HIBERNATING
STAGE:**
Pupa

FLIGHT PERIOD:
Early to mid-
summer

**CATERPILLAR FOOD
PLANTS:**
Most low-growing
plants, trees and
shrubs

This moth is common throughout most of
Europe except N Scandinavia and Scotland. It
can be found almost anywhere, but it is
probably commonest in cultivated areas such
as parks and gardens. Although it is not often
seen during the day, the moths are easily
attracted by bright lights at night. The
caterpillar varies in colour from green to
brown and has a small hump at the tail. It
pupates in an underground cocoon.

caterpillar

NOCTUIDAE (OWLET MOTHS)

Old Lady
Mormo maura

ID FACT FILE

WINGSPAN:
6–7 cm

DESCRIPTION:
Dark grey-brown
with darker mark-
ings; hindwings
edged with pale
brown. Female
larger

**HIBERNATING
STAGE:**
Caterpillar

FLIGHT PERIOD:
Mid- to late
summer

**CATERPILLAR FOOD
PLANTS:**
Dock (*Rumex*) at
first, changing to
various trees and
shrubs in spring

This large moth is locally common throughout
central and S Europe, and also most of the
British Isles. It prefers open woodland and
hedgerows, but can sometimes be found in
gardens. During the day the adult hides away
in dark places such as hollow trees, sometimes
coming into houses to shelter. The caterpillar
feeds at first on low-growing plants, but after
hibernation moves up to feed on shrubs and
trees. Pupation takes place underground.

caterpillar

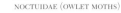

NOCTUIDAE (OWLET MOTHS)

| J | F | M | A | M | J |
| J | A | S | O | N | D |

Gothic
Naenia typica

ID FACT FILE

WINGSPAN:
4–4.7 cm

DESCRIPTION:
Forewings
mottled in light
and dark brown-
ish-grey, veins
picked out in
white; hindwings
pale fawn,
almost white
near body. Sexes
alike

**HIBERNATING
STAGE:**
Caterpillar

FLIGHT PERIOD:
Early to mid-
summer

**CATERPILLAR FOOD
PLANTS:**
Many low-growing
plants, trees and
shrubs

A common moth everywhere except
N Scandinavia, although it is not often found
very high up in the hills, preferring woodland
edges, hedgerows and gardens in lowland
areas. It is difficult to spot during the day, but
at night it is very fond of privet (*Ligustrum*)
flowers. The pale brown caterpillar feeds on a
huge variety of different plants, and when fully
grown makes a flimsy cocoon underground in
which to pupate.

caterpillar

NOCTUIDAE (OWLET MOTHS)

J	F	M	A	M	J
J	A	S	O	N	D

Large Yellow Underwing
Noctua pronuba

ID FACT FILE

WINGSPAN:
5–6 cm

DESCRIPTION:
Forewings mid-brown with
1 darker and
1 paler spot near the middle, and another darker spot near the tip; hindwings bright yellow with a black band near the edges. Female larger and paler

HIBERNATING STAGE:
Caterpillar

FLIGHT PERIOD:
Early summer to early autumn

CATERPILLAR FOOD PLANTS:
Many low-growing plants

This very common moth is found throughout Europe, and can be seen almost everywhere, especially in gardens and other cultivated land where it may sometimes become a pest. It is easily attracted to flowers and bright lights at night, but in the warmer south it may become dormant during the hottest weather. The caterpillar may be green or brown; it feeds at night, hiding underground during the day, and pupates below ground when fully grown.

caterpillar

NOCTUIDAE (OWLET MOTHS)

Hebrew Character
Orthosia gothica

ID FACT FILE

WINGSPAN:
3.3–3.8 cm

DESCRIPTION:
Forewings pale
brownish-grey
with a marbled
pattern and a
clearly defined
dark spot near
the middle; hind-
wings very pale
brown. Sexes
alike

**HIBERNATING
STAGE:**
Pupa

FLIGHT PERIOD:
Early to mid-
spring

**CATERPILLAR FOOD
PLANTS:**
Many low-growing
plants, trees and
shrubs

A very common moth throughout Europe,
found almost everywhere, even in the
mountains, although it is probably commonest
in wooded and cultivated areas. As it flies very
early in the year, there are few suitable flowers
available and it is most likely to be seen feeding
from sallow (*Salix*) blossom at night. The pale
green caterpillar is well camouflaged, and when
fully grown burrows underground to pupate.

caterpillar

J	F	M	A	M	J
J	A	S	O	N	D

Pine Beauty
Panolis flammea

ID FACT FILE

WINGSPAN:
3–3.8 cm

DESCRIPTION:
Forewings
marbled with
orange-brown
and white, with
a clear whitish
spot near the
middle; hind-
wings pale
brown. Sexes
alike

**HIBERNATING
STAGE:**
Pupa

FLIGHT PERIOD:
Early to mid-
spring

**CATERPILLAR FOOD
PLANTS:**
Pine (*Pinus*)
trees

This moth is common throughout most of
Europe, although it is rather rare in Ireland and
absent from N Scandinavia. Because the adult
flies early in the year it is most likely to be seen
feeding from sallow (*Salix*) flowers at night. The
caterpillars live in groups and can sometimes
become serious pests. When fully grown they
pupate in a flimsy cocoon either under the bark
or on the ground amongst fallen leaves.

caterpillar

NOCTUIDAE (OWLET MOTHS)

J	F	M	A	M	J
J	A	S	O	N	D

Angle Shades
Phlogophora meticulosa

ID FACT FILE

WINGSPAN:
4.5–5 cm

DESCRIPTION:
Easily recognised by its crumpled-looking wings and large triangular patch in the middle of the forewings; hindwings very pale with fine, dark lines. Sexes alike

HIBERNATING STAGE:
Pupa or caterpillar

FLIGHT PERIOD:
Spring to autumn

CATERPILLAR FOOD PLANTS:
Many low-growing plants and shrubs

This moth is common throughout Europe except N Scandinavia and is often seen in gardens. There are two basic colour forms of the adult, olive-green and pinkish-brown, and the wings look crumpled when it is resting, with the result that it looks like an old leaf. There may be several overlapping broods each year. The caterpillar can also be either green or brown, and pupates in a very flimsy cocoon on the ground.

caterpillar

NOCTUIDAE (OWLET MOTHS)

J	F	M	A	M	J
J	A	S	O	N	D

Green Silver-lines
Pseudoips fagana

This little moth is easily recognised, and is common throughout northern and central Europe and some southern parts. It occurs mainly in beech woods, quite high in the mountains, and also hedgerows, but it is very difficult to find. The caterpillar, too, is very well camouflaged, and when fully grown pupates in a boat-shaped cocoon which may be under a growing leaf or down at ground level amongst dead leaves.

ID FACT FILE

WINGSPAN:
3.2–4 cm

DESCRIPTION:
Forewings diagonally striped with green and white, edged with red-dish-orange (male) or white (female). Hind-wings white, tinted with yellow on the male

HIBERNATING STAGE:
Pupa

FLIGHT PERIOD:
Early summer

CATERPILLAR FOOD PLANTS:
Beech (*Fagus*), oak (*Quercus*) and birch (*Betula*)

caterpillar

female

NOCTUIDAE (OWLET MOTHS)

Herald
Scoliopteryx libatrix

ID FACT FILE

WINGSPAN:
4–4.5 cm

DESCRIPTION:
Pale reddish-brown; forewings deeply scalloped, with orange-brown patches and white lines. Sexes alike

HIBERNATING STAGE:
Adult

FLIGHT PERIOD:
Late summer to early autumn and spring

CATERPILLAR FOOD PLANTS:
Poplar (*Populus*) and willow (*Salix*)

This common moth can be found everywhere in Europe, preferring damp, open places, and also parks and gardens up to around 2000 m. It is usually seen feeding from flowers such as ivy (*Hedera*), but can sometimes be attracted to very ripe fruit. Occasionally it can be found trying to hibernate in a shed or other outhouse. The caterpillar is extremely well camouflaged, and when fully grown makes a white cocoon amongst the leaves in which to pupate.

caterpillar

NOCTUIDAE (OWLET MOTHS)

| J | F | M | A | M | J |
| J | A | S | O | N | D |

Swordgrass
Xylena exsoleta

ID FACT FILE

WINGSPAN:
5.5–6.5 cm

DESCRIPTION:
Pale straw
colouring,
forewings with
darker edges and
2 large darker
spots near the
middle. Female
generally darker

**HIBERNATING
STAGE:**
Adult

FLIGHT PERIOD:
Early autumn and
spring

**CATERPILLAR FOOD
PLANTS:**
Many low-growing
plants and some
trees

This is quite a common moth throughout
Europe except for N Scandinavia. It prefers
damp moorland and peat-bogs, also open
woodland and cultivated land. When at rest it
wraps its wings tightly around its body and
looks rather like a broken twig or piece of
wood, making it very hard to find; but at night
it may be seen feeding from flowers such as ivy
(*Hedera*) and sallow (*Salix*). The caterpillar
pupates underground.

caterpillar

| J | F | M | A | M | J |
| J | A | S | O | N | D |

Pale Tussock
Dasychira pudibunda

ID FACT FILE

WINGSPAN:
5–6.5 cm

DESCRIPTION:
Forewings very
pale brownish-
grey with darker
band across the
middle; hind-
wings almost
white. Female
much larger and
paler

**HIBERNATING
STAGE:**
Pupa

FLIGHT PERIOD:
Late spring

**CATERPILLAR FOOD
PLANTS:**
Many trees and
shrubs

This is a common moth over most of northern
and central Europe except Scotland, preferring
woodland areas, parks and gardens, up to
around 1000 m. The extraordinary hairy
caterpillar is usually pale yellow or green, with
four prominent tufts of white or yellow hair on
its back, between which black bands can be
seen when it curls up; there is a long pink tuft
at the tail end. It pupates in a silk cocoon near
the ground.

female

male

LYMANTRIIDAE (TUSSOCK MOTHS)

Brown Tail
Euproctis chrysorrhoea

ID FACT FILE

WINGSPAN:
3–4.3 cm

DESCRIPTION:
Male pure white, with completely brown abdomen; female similar, but larger, with abdomen brown only at the tip

HIBERNATING STAGE:
Caterpillar

FLIGHT PERIOD:
Mid-summer

CATERPILLAR FOOD PLANTS:
Many trees and shrubs

This is a common and well-known moth throughout central and S Europe, including S England. It can be found mainly in woodland and hedgerows, but also parks, gardens and orchards. The female lays large clusters of eggs and covers them with hairs from the tip of her abdomen. The caterpillars live together in a communal silk tent until fully grown, and their hairs may cause an extremely painful rash, sometimes even temporary blindness.

caterpillar

male

LYMANTRIIDAE (TUSSOCK MOTHS)

Vapourer
Orgyia antiqua

ID FACT FILE

WINGSPAN:
2.5–3 cm

DESCRIPTION:
Male dark orange-brown with single white spot on each forewing. Female grey, wingless

HIBERNATING STAGE:
Egg

FLIGHT PERIOD:
Mid-summer to early autumn; 2 or 3 broods

CATERPILLAR FOOD PLANTS:
Most trees and shrubs

A common moth throughout most of Europe except S Spain. It prefers woodland, parks and gardens, and the males can often be seen flying during the afternoon in search of females, who never leave their cocoons, laying their eggs on the outside of this. The hairy caterpillar is dark grey with red spots and four dense clumps of yellow hairs along its back which may cause a slight rash. It can sometimes become a pest when found in large numbers.

right: female with eggs on cocoon

below: male

J	F	M	A	M	J
J	A	S	O	N	D

Gypsy Moth
Lymantria dispar

ID FACT FILE

WINGSPAN:
3.5–5.5 cm

DESCRIPTION:
Male pale brownish-grey with a wavy pattern in dark brown; female much larger and very pale

HIBERNATING STAGE:
Egg

FLIGHT PERIOD:
Mid- to late summer

CATERPILLAR FOOD PLANTS:
Many deciduous trees

This is a very well-known moth, found throughout most of Europe except N Scandinavia and the British Isles. It normally occurs in woodlands and orchards and can be a serious pest, sometimes completely stripping trees. Males fly during the day, but the female rarely flies far, and covers her eggs with hairs from her abdomen. The caterpillar is grey with a black line down the back, and blue, red and yellow hairy spots.

male

female

LYMANTRIIDAE (TUSSOCK MOTHS)

Black Arches
Lymantria monacha

ID FACT FILE

WINGSPAN:
3.5–5.5 cm

DESCRIPTION:
Male forewings
white with a wavy
black pattern;
hindwings pale
smoky brown,
fringed with black
and white.
Female much
larger and more
heavily marked,
with a striped
abdomen

HIBERNATING STAGE:
Egg

FLIGHT PERIOD:
Mid- to late
summer

CATERPILLAR FOOD PLANTS:
Pine (*Pinus*), oak
(*Quercus*) and
birch (*Betula*)

This moth is fairly common throughout most of
northern and central Europe, except for the
very far north. In the British Isles it is found
only in S England and parts of Wales. It
prefers woodland, both pine and deciduous,
and can sometimes be a serious pest. The
caterpillar is greyish-brown marked with black
spots and lines, and quite hairy. It pupates in a
cocoon hidden away under bark.

caterpillar

male

ARCTIIDAE (TIGER AND FOOTMAN MOTHS)

Garden Tiger
Arctia caja

ID FACT FILE

J	F	M	A	M	J
J	A	S	O	N	D

WINGSPAN:
4.5–6.5 cm

DESCRIPTION:
Very variable. Forewings usually white with dark brown spots; hindwings red to yellow with blue-centred black spots. Female larger

HIBERNATING STAGE:
Caterpillar

FLIGHT PERIOD:
Early to mid-summer

CATERPILLAR FOOD PLANTS:
Nettle (*Urtica*), dandelion (*Taraxacum*) and many other low-growing plants

LOOKALIKES:
Cream-spot Tiger (p.230)

A very common moth throughout Europe, and can be found almost anywhere that suitable food plants can be found. It is very variable in appearance, so much so, in fact, that it is rare to find two individuals with identical markings. The densely hairy caterpillars can be seen feeding up in the spring, particularly on sunny days, and are commonly known as 'woolly bears'. Pupation takes place within a white silk cocoon.

caterpillar

ARCTIIDAE (TIGER AND FOOTMAN MOTHS)

J	F	M	A	M	J
J	A	S	O	N	D

Cream-spot Tiger
Arctia villica

ID FACT FILE

WINGSPAN:
4.5–6 cm

DESCRIPTION:
Variable.
Forewings dark
brown with
cream spots;
hindwings orange
with brown
spots. Female
larger

**HIBERNATING
STAGE:**
Caterpillar

FLIGHT PERIOD:
Late spring

**CATERPILLAR FOOD
PLANTS:**
Dandelion
(*Taraxacum*),
dock (*Rumex*)

LOOKALIKES:
Garden Tiger
(p.229)

This moth is found throughout most of
Europe, but it is not quite as common as the
Garden Tiger. It prefers woodlands and
hedgerows, and also sheltered grassy areas.
Like most other Tiger moths, it is readily
attracted to lights, but can also sometimes be
seen flying during the day. Fully grown
caterpillars can be seen sunning themselves in
the spring, and they can move across open
ground at quite a speed.

caterpillar

ARCTIIDAE (TIGER AND FOOTMAN MOTHS)

J	F	M	A	M	J
J	A	S	O	N	D

Scarlet Tiger
Callimorpha dominula

ID FACT FILE

WINGSPAN:
4.5–5.5 cm

DESCRIPTION:
Extremely vari-
able: forewings,
white and yellow
spots on black
ground; hind-
wings, black
spots on red to
yellow ground.
Sexes alike

**HIBERNATING
STAGE:**
Caterpillar

FLIGHT PERIOD:
Late spring to
late summer

**CATERPILLAR FOOD
PLANTS:**
Wide variety of
low-growing
plants, but par-
ticularly nettle
(*Urtica*) and
comfrey
(*Symphytum*)

This moth is found throughout the more
temperate parts of Europe and Asia, though
very locally in some countries; it has a strong
preference for damp habitats, such as river
banks and surrounding wet meadows. This
is one of the very few Tiger moths that have
well-developed adult mouthparts, and the
moths can be seen flying during the day, as
well as at night, from flower to flower in a
search for nectar.

caterpillar

ARCTIIDAE (TIGER AND FOOTMAN MOTHS)

J	F	M	A	M	J
J	A	S	O	N	D

Clouded Buff

Diacrisia sannio

ID FACT FILE

WINGSPAN:
3.5–4.5 cm

DESCRIPTION:
The male has a
reddish-brown
spot in the
middle of yellow
forewings, and a
dark border to
cream or white
hindwings. The
female is similar-
ly marked but
much darker,
and the forewing
spot is less
obvious

**HIBERNATING
STAGE:**
Caterpillar

FLIGHT PERIOD:
Early summer in
the north, late
spring to
mid-summer in
the south

**CATERPILLAR FOOD
PLANTS:**
Wide range of
low-growing
plants

This moth is common throughout Europe, but
prefers open grassland such as heaths, moors
and downland. Males are attracted to lights at
night, but can also be seen flying during the
day as they search for females, who fly only at
night. There is only one brood each year in the
north, two in the south. The hairy caterpillar is
reddish-brown with a cream stripe down the
back. It pupates in a flimsy cocoon amongst
leaf-litter.

female   male

ARCTIIDAE (TIGER AND FOOTMAN MOTHS)

Common Footman
Eilema lurideola

ID FACT FILE

J	F	M	A	M	J
J	A	S	O	N	D

WINGSPAN:
2.8–3.5 cm

DESCRIPTION:
Forewings pale
grey with a
narrow margin of
cream along the
leading edge;
hindwings white,
tinged with
cream

**HIBERNATING
STAGE:**
Caterpillar

FLIGHT PERIOD:
Early to
mid-summer

**CATERPILLAR FOOD
PLANTS:**
Lichens. Will
accept foliage of
various plants in
captivity

As its name suggests, this is a common moth,
found throughout Europe except the far north
of the region; it normally prefers wooded areas
and hedgerows. Like most other footman
moths, the wings are folded flat over its back
when at rest, but the moth is most often seen
when it is attracted to lights at night, or
sometimes when flying round flowers such as
thistles (*Carduus*) at dusk. The cocoon is
usually made in a bark crevice.

caterpillar

J	F	M	A	M	J
J	A	S	O	N	D

Wood Tiger
Parasemia plantaginis

ID FACT FILE

WINGSPAN:
3.2–3.8 cm

DESCRIPTION:
Variable pattern of black markings on white or cream forewings; yellow hindwings. Female is more heavily marked, especially on the hindwings, and the yellow may vary to reddish

HIBERNATING STAGE:
Caterpillar

FLIGHT PERIOD:
Early to mid-summer

CATERPILLAR FOOD PLANTS:
Wide range of low-growing plants

This moth is common throughout most of Europe and, despite its name, it is found in open spaces such as heaths, moorland and downland, as well as open woodland. It flies both at night and during the day, when it keeps quite close to the ground. The caterpillar is black, and densely covered with long black hairs and shorter red-brown hairs. It makes a cocoon in the spring amongst the leaves of the plant on which it has been feeding.

left male
right female

J	F	M	A	M	J
J	A	S	O	N	D

Ruby Tiger
Phragmatobia fuliginosa

ID FACT FILE

WINGSPAN:
3.4–4 cm

DESCRIPTION:
Dark reddish-brown, hindwings mainly black. Two small black spots on each wing. Female larger

HIBERNATING STAGE:
Caterpillar

FLIGHT PERIOD:
Late spring to early summer, also late summer to early autumn in the south

CATERPILLAR FOOD PLANTS:
Many low-growing plants such as dock (*Rumex*)

This fairly common moth is found almost everywhere in Europe, although in some areas it is only locally common. It can be seen in most habitats, particularly open woodland and meadows, anywhere that suitable food plants can be found. There are two broods each year in the south, but normally only one in the cooler north. In spring, after hibernation, the fully grown caterpillar pupates in a cocoon on the ground, usually amongst leaf-litter.

caterpillar

ARCTIIDAE (TIGER AND FOOTMAN MOTHS)

J	F	M	A	M	J
J	A	S	O	N	D

White Ermine
Spilosoma lubricepeda

ID FACT FILE

WINGSPAN:
3–4.2 cm

DESCRIPTION:
Variable pattern of small black spots on white ground. Easily recognised from any other white moth by the yellow abdomen. Sexes alike.

HIBERNATING STAGE:
Pupa

FLIGHT PERIOD:
Late spring to early summer

CATERPILLAR FOOD PLANTS:
Almost any low-growing plant

This very common moth is found almost everywhere in Europe, and in virtually every kind of habitat, although it does have a preference for open spaces. It is easily attracted to lights at night, and this is probably when it is most often seen. The caterpillar makes a cocoon close to the ground amongst leaves or leaf-litter. There is occasionally a partial second brood in the autumn, when the climate is favourable.

caterpillar

ARCTIIDAE (TIGER AND FOOTMAN MOTHS)

J	F	M	A	M	J
J	A	S	O	N	D

Cinnabar

Tyria jacobaeae

ID FACT FILE

WINGSPAN:
3.2–4.2 cm

DESCRIPTION:
Forewings black
with a red line
close to the lead-
ing edge and
2 red spots;
hindwings red,
edged with black.
Sexes alike

**HIBERNATING
STAGE:**
Pupa

FLIGHT PERIOD:
Late spring to
early summer

**CATERPILLAR FOOD
PLANTS:**
Ragwort
(*Senecio*)

A moth of open places, such as heathland, and
downland, and found through most of Europe,
although it is not abundantly common. Mainly
a night-flying species, it is easily disturbed
during the day, when its weak flight and bright
colours make it easy to see. The bright colours
of both adult and caterpillar advertise the fact
that this species is distasteful to birds. The
caterpillar makes a flimsy cocoon on or under
the ground.

caterpillar

CTENUCHIDAE (CTENUCHID MOTHS)

J	F	M	A	M	J
J	A	S	O	N	D

Nine-spotted
Syntomis phegea

ID FACT FILE

WINGSPAN:
3.5–4 cm

DESCRIPTION:
Black with a blue
sheen, with 6
greyish spots on
each forewing, 3,
sometimes 2, on
each hindwing; 2
yellow bands on
body. Sexes
alike

**HIBERNATING
STAGE:**
Caterpillar

FLIGHT PERIOD:
Early to
mid-summer

**CATERPILLAR FOOD
PLANTS:**
Dandelion
(*Taraxacum*) and
many other low-
growing plants

LOOKALIKES:
Variable Burnet
(p.242)

This little moth is locally common in S Europe,
except Spain, and also some parts of central
Europe. It is a day-flying species and prefers
dry, sunny grasslands and open woodland, up
to around 2000 m. It is easily confused with
the Variable Burnet. The caterpillars hibernate
in a silk tent, separating in the spring when
almost fully grown. They pupate on the ground
amongst leaf-litter in a flimsy cocoon
decorated with their hairs.

caterpillar

SESIIDAE (CLEARWING MOTHS)

J	F	M	A	M	J
J	A	S	O	N	D

Hornet Moth
Sesia apiformis

ID FACT FILE

WINGSPAN:
3.5–4.5 cm

DESCRIPTION:
Wings transparent, edged yellowish-brown; body striped yellow and dark brown. Sexes alike

HIBERNATING STAGE:
Caterpillar

FLIGHT PERIOD:
Late spring to mid-summer

CATERPILLAR FOOD PLANTS:
Poplar (*Populus*), inside lower trunk and roots

This moth is found throughout most of Europe, except Scotland and N Scandinavia and Finland, and is often common locally. It prefers the edges and clearings of damp woodland and hedgerows, where it can sometimes be seen sitting on a tree trunk in the morning. The creamy-yellow caterpillar takes two years to develop and usually pupates just under the bark of its tree. Empty pupa cases can sometimes be seen sticking out of the trunk in early summer.

empty pupa

PSYCHIDAE (BAGWORMS)

J	F	M	A	M	J
J	A	S	O	N	D

Bagworm
Canephora unicolor

ID FACT FILE

WINGSPAN:
2.5 cm

DESCRIPTION:
Males dark
brown; females
wingless

**HIBERNATING
STAGE:**
Caterpillar

FLIGHT PERIOD:
Early to late
summer

**CATERPILLAR FOOD
PLANTS:**
Various grasses,
also broom
(*Cytisus*)

This is the largest of the 200 or so species of
bagworm to be found in Europe, and is locally
common almost everywhere except the British
Isles and the far north. The name comes from
the protective case made by the caterpillar.
Only the male has wings, and can sometimes
be seen flying during the afternoon or early
evening. The female never leaves the case
(some other species do not even have legs!)
and lays her eggs on the outside.

female caterpillar

adult male

male caterpillar

ZYGAENIDAE (BURNETS AND FORESTERS)

J	F	M	A	M	J
J	A	S	O	N	D

Forester
Adscita statices

ID FACT FILE

WINGSPAN:
2.5–3 cm

DESCRIPTION:
Forewings dark metallic green; hindwings pale grey, slightly transparent. Sexes alike except for antennae

HIBERNATING STAGE:
Caterpillar

FLIGHT PERIOD:
Late spring to mid-summer, depending on locality

CATERPILLAR FOOD PLANTS:
Sorrel (*Rumex*)

This common little moth is found throughout most of Europe except the far north. It is a day-flying species preferring damp meadows and open woodland up to around 1500 m, and is strongly attracted to flowers. The caterpillar is very pale yellow or green and covered with brown warts producing short hairs. When very small it lives under the surface of a leaf; when larger it emerges to eat the lower surface only, leaving the little 'windows' behind.

male antenna

female antenna

ZYGAENIDAE (BURNETS AND FORESTERS)

J	F	M	A	M	J
J	A	S	O	N	D

Variable Burnet
Zygaena ephialtes

This moth is found throughout most of central and S Europe, where it prefers dry, sunny grassland and woodland edges up to around 1500 m. It is a sun-loving species, with a slow, lazy flight, and strongly attracted to flowers. There are many different colour forms, which can be a little confusing. In some areas the caterpillar may take two years to develop, and when fully grown it pupates in a tough cocoon close to the ground.

ID FACT FILE

WINGSPAN:
3–4.5 cm

DESCRIPTION:
Black with a slightly blue sheen and spotted with red, red and white, yellow or yellow and white; only 1 band of red or yellow on the body. Sexes alike

HIBERNATING STAGE:
Caterpillar

FLIGHT PERIOD:
Early to late summer

CATERPILLAR FOOD PLANTS:
Crown vetch (*Coronilla*) and related plants

LOOKALIKES:
Nine-spotted (p.238)

caterpillar

ZYGAENIDAE (BURNETS AND FORESTERS)

J	F	M	A	M	J
J	A	S	O	N	D

Six-spot Burnet
Zygaena filipendulae

ID FACT FILE

WINGSPAN:
3–3.8 cm

DESCRIPTION:
Black with a bluish sheen and 6 red spots on each forewing; hindwings red with black edges. Sexes alike

HIBERNATING STAGE:
Caterpillar

FLIGHT PERIOD:
Early summer

CATERPILLAR FOOD PLANTS:
Bird's-foot-trefoil (*Lotus*)

This is probably the commonest of the burnet moths, and is found throughout most of Europe except the far north and S Spain. It prefers flowery meadows and other grasslands, up to around 2000 m. The caterpillar is pale green with black spots and a black head, and pupates in a straw-coloured cocoon high up on a grass stem. Both adult and caterpillar can produce a poisonous liquid from special glands to warn off predators.

mating pair

Six-spot Burnet
exuding toxins

J	F	M	A	M	J
J	A	S	O	N	D

Transparent Burnet
Zygaena purpuralis

ID FACT FILE

WINGSPAN:
2.8–3.5 cm

DESCRIPTION:
Forewings black
with 3 long red
streaks; hind-
wings red, finely
edged black. All
wings slightly
transparent

**HIBERNATING
STAGE:**
Caterpillar

FLIGHT PERIOD:
Early to
mid-summer

**CATERPILLAR FOOD
PLANTS:**
Thyme (*Thymus*)

This moth is fairly common throughout most of
central and S Europe except Spain and
W France; in the British Isles it is found in
Ireland and W Scotland. Like other burnet
moths, it flies during the day, and prefers
flowery grasslands in full sun, wherever the
food plant grows, up to around 2000 m. When
fully grown the caterpillar pupates in a tough
straw-coloured cocoon hidden amongst leaves
close to the ground.

caterpillar

COSSIDAE (CARPENTERS)

| J | F | M | A | M | J |
| J | A | S | O | N | D |

Goat Moth
Cossus cossus

ID FACT FILE

WINGSPAN:
7–9.5 cm

DESCRIPTION:
Pale greyish-brown, lighter near the body, patterned with small dark streaks across the wings. Female much larger

HIBERNATING STAGE:
Caterpillar

FLIGHT PERIOD:
Early summer

CATERPILLAR FOOD PLANTS:
Many trees, especially poplar (*Populus*) and willow (*Salix*)

This large moth is fairly common throughout most of Europe except the far north. It prefers deciduous woodland and sometimes old orchards that are no longer looked after, and can be found up to around 2000 m. The caterpillar is pinkish-yellow with a red-brown back, and smells strongly, rather like a goat. It bores into tree trunks and takes around three years to complete its development. It pupates in a cocoon, often still in the tree.

caterpillar

COSSIDAE (CARPENTERS)

Leopard Moth
Zeuzera pyrina

J	F	M	A	M	J
J	A	S	O	N	D

ID FACT FILE

WINGSPAN:
4.5–7.5 cm

DESCRIPTION:
White, slightly
transparent, with
black spots and
yellow veins.
Female much
larger with a
long, harmless,
egg-laying tube
(ovipositor)

**HIBERNATING
STAGE:**
Caterpillar

FLIGHT PERIOD:
Mid- to late
summer

**CATERPILLAR FOOD
PLANTS:**
Many deciduous
trees

This is a common moth throughout central and
S Europe, and also S England. It can be found
wherever trees grow: deciduous woodlands,
orchards, gardens, and even streets if they have
trees along them. The caterpillar is a dark
cream colour with black, bristly spots and a
brown head. It tunnels through the wood of
many trees, usually just below the bark, and
takes two or three years before pupating within
its burrow.

caterpillar

male

HEPIALIDAE (SWIFT MOTHS)

J	F	M	A	M	J
J	A	S	O	N	D

Ghost Moth

Hepialus humuli

ID FACT FILE

WINGSPAN:
4.5–7 cm

DESCRIPTION:
Male, plain
silvery white;
female, pale
straw colour with
slightly darker
streaks along the
forewings

**HIBERNATING
STAGE:**
Caterpillar

FLIGHT PERIOD:
Early to
mid-summer

**CATERPILLAR FOOD
PLANTS:**
Roots of various
grasses

This moth is common throughout most of
Europe, and can be found in most types of
grassland, mainly in the lowlands but also up to
around 2000 m. These moths fly mainly at
dusk, the males hovering close to the ground in
one spot, waiting for the females. After mating
the female drops her eggs while flying. The
caterpillar is pale yellowish-brown with dark
brown spots. Pupation takes place in an
underground chamber.

female

male

HEPIALIDAE (SWIFT MOTHS)

J	F	M	A	M	J
J	A	S	O	N	D

Common Swift
Hepialus luplinus

ID FACT FILE

WINGSPAN:
2.7–4 cm

DESCRIPTION:
Dark brown with white patches on the forewings. Female larger and paler

HIBERNATING STAGE:
Caterpillar

FLIGHT PERIOD:
Late spring

CATERPILLAR FOOD PLANTS:
Roots of various grasses and many other plants

A very common moth throughout most of Europe except the far north, and found mainly in meadows, gardens and other cultivated land. Like the Ghost Moth, the female drops her eggs while flying, but chooses her sites with more care. The caterpillar is pale brown with slightly darker spots, and in some colder areas it may take two years to develop. Through eating the roots of so many different plants it sometimes becomes a pest.

male

female

HEPIALIDAE (SWIFT MOTHS)

J	F	M	A	M	J
J	A	S	O	N	D

Orange Swift
Hepialis sylvina

ID FACT FILE

WINGSPAN:
2.7–4.5 cm

DESCRIPTION:
Male orange-brown with white-edged dark brown streaks on the forewings. Female dark greyish-brown, patterned with white lines

HIBERNATING STAGE:
Caterpillar

FLIGHT PERIOD:
Mid- to late summer

CATERPILLAR FOOD PLANTS:
Roots of many grasses and other plants

This moth is fairly common across most of central and S Europe, preferring most types of grassland, gardens and cultivated land, mainly in lowland areas. It can usually be seen flying around at dusk. The female drops her eggs while flying. The caterpillar is greyish-white with two rows of bristly black warts, and sometimes becomes a serious pest. When fully grown it pupates in a cigar-shaped cocoon underground.

male

female

INDEX

Numbers in brackets indicate cross references in the text.

WHAT NEXT?

Further reading

As mentioned earlier, this book has been written mainly for beginners, so eventually you may want to expand your knowledge. The best way to set about this is to visit your local library, and have a look at the books they have available. Many books have been written about butterflies and moths, but many of them are no longer printed, so a trip to a second-hand bookshop may be worthwhile. To learn more about butterflies and how to keep them, try and find a copy of *Butterflies* by E.B. Ford (published in the New Naturalist series by Collins). A more extensive identification guide to butterflies is *Collins Field Guide to the Butterflies of Britain and Europe* by Tom Tolman and Richard Lewington. For moths, try *Moths of the British Isles* by R. South (Warne). In addition, gardening and photography magazines often have articles containing useful information, including places to visit and where to purchase equipment and other supplies.

Joining a society

Societies can be very useful and give you a chance to meet other people who share your interests. The **Amateur Entomologists' Society** (www.ex.ac.uk/bugclub/main.html) produces lots of different leaflets and booklets on all aspects of keeping and studying insects, including butterflies and moths, and is probably the best to join. Write to the General Secretary, The Amateur Entomologists' Society, PO Box 8774, London SW7 5ZG. **Butterfly Conservation** (www.butterfly-conservation.org) is also very good, and has many conservation projects that you may be able to help with. Write to them at Manor Yard, East Lulworth, Wareham, Dorset, BH20 5QP (tel. 0870 774 4309).

Finally, if you have a Butterfly Centre near you then it might be worth paying them a visit, as you may be lucky enough to find someone on the staff who will be willing to give you help or advice.

 **Collins**

If you have enjoyed this book, why not have a look at some of the other titles in the WILD GUIDE series?

Birds	0-00-717792-5
Wild Flowers	0-00-717793-3
Insects	0-00-717795-X
Night Sky	0-00-717790-9
Night Sky Starfinder	0-00-717791-7
Weather	0-00-716072-0
Seashore	0-00-716071-2
Garden Birds	0-00-717789-5
Mushrooms	0-00-719150-2
Trees	0-00-719152-9
Rocks and Minerals	0-00-717794-1
British Wildlife	0-00-719172-3

Other titles of interest from Collins:

Collins Field Guide Butterflies by Tom Tolman,
    Illustrated by Richard Lewington 0-00-718991-5
Collins Nature Guide Butterflies and Moths by H.
    Hofmann and T. Marktanner 0-00-220029-5
Complete British Insects by Michael Chinery
    0-00-717966-9

To order any of these titles please call **0870 787 1732**.

For further information about Collins books visit our website: **www.collins.co.uk**